RAISED BED GARDENING FOR BEGINNERS

TRANSFORM YOUR GARDEN INTO A THRIVING OASIS WITH EXPERT TIPS ON CHOOSING BED TYPE, SOIL PREPARATION, MASTERING PEST CONTROL, AND MORE!

MICHELLE M DAMIANI

TABLE OF CONTENTS

Me standing next to garden after helping my father put tents over the plants to protect from frost that was in the forecast for the next morning. Circa late 1970s.

My brother with our two dogs in front of our garden. Circa late 1970s.

INTRODUCTION

Let's take a break and slow down for a moment. We live in a fast-paced world where technology and urban landscapes dominate. A timeless and therapeutic art form connects us with nature and nurtures our well-being—gardening. Beyond the beauty of vibrant flowers, bountiful vegetables, and buzzing bees, this horticultural practice has the power to rejuvenate our bodies, minds, and souls. The simple act of gardening can be a profound catalyst for improved health and vitality.

There have been countless studies documenting the positive impact of spending time outdoors and gardening. Stress is the silent killer of our time. Emotional stress has been linked to six of the leading causes of death in the United States. Gardening, on the other hand, reduces stress and anxiety. Time in nature is good for the lungs, digestion, and immune system. It reduces heart rate and let's not forget all the benefits of being outside soaking up vitamin D from the sun! Gardening allows us to ground ourselves and offers a much-needed respite from the daily noise life throws into our paths.

When my brother and I were growing up, my parents decided at some point that we needed a garden—a big one! This is where my parents learned everything they could about how to grow and preserve food. There were a few failed crops in the beginning but there were many more successful crops that followed. My brother and I were expected to help in the garden. We had to weed, help seed, and help harvest. While my father played a vital role in shaping us into patient, caring, and knowledgeable gardeners, my mother was equally instrumental in the art of canning, transforming our harvest into sauces, salsas, jams, and pickles. When she finished canning for the season our basement shelves were a beautiful display of our gardening success. We learned valuable lessons that extended beyond our fenced-in yard.

As time rolled forward, the garden became too much for our parents. My brother and I moved out and started our own families and gardens. Then life took a sorrowful turn when my mother unexpectedly passed. My father's partner in gardening was no longer here. My father was older now and had trouble with the physical demands of tending a garden. So, he stopped gardening for a while. He kept up his compost pile because he says you always need good dirt. Years later, he found that raised beds could bring the garden up to his level, allowing him to get back to doing what he loved, of course on a much smaller scale.

My parents planted a passion for gardening and a curiosity to explore the possibilities that gardening offers within me. Maybe you have wanted to try gardening and connect with the earth to create your own haven of nourishment but just don't know where to start, or you might have encountered challenges and doubts, questioning whether you possess the elusive green thumb required to thrive in the world of gardening. Set aside your worries! This comprehensive guide will help you to cultivate your own green sanctuary, no matter how small or large your slice of paradise may be. It's an invitation for you to discover your roots and embrace the healing power of your outdoor space! I will introduce to you the 6 Ps of raised bed gardening: Planning, Preparing, Planting, Parenting, Pairing, and Protection.

Embracing this new hobby means creating a healthier lifestyle for you and your family and a connection to what you are consuming. Instead of wasting time and gas going to the grocery store for overpriced vegetables that may or may not be chemical-free, remember that your backyard holds the potential for a more organic and economical alternative.

Are you prepared to start this life-changing journey? Then let's dig deep, plant our intentions, and watch as our dreams take root and bloom.

1

PLANNING FOR SUCCESSFUL RAISED BEDS

Are you ready to discover the benefits of raised bed gardening and how it can transform the way you grow and cultivate your garden? By the time we reach the conclusion of this chapter, you will possess a comprehensive understanding of the key factors to consider when selecting the ideal location for your raised beds. Together, we will explore the unique needs of plants, including their sunlight requirements, shade considerations, and even water management. Armed with this knowledge, you will be able to meticulously plan and create your raised beds to optimize the growth and well-being of your beloved plants.

Did you know that a single food garden spanning 200 to 399 square feet, requiring just one to two hours of work per week, has the remarkable potential to sustain four people for an entire year? Astonishing, isn't it? According to gardening statistics from 2021, the average return on investment in food gardening reached a staggering 757%. This astounding figure highlights the immense rewards that await those who embark on the journey of growing their own food. Imagine the profound satisfaction of plucking ripe tomatoes from the vine, savoring the delicate sweetness of homegrown strawberries, and relishing the crispness of freshly picked lettuce. Raised bed gardening not only nourishes our bodies but also nourishes our connection with nature.

As we progress together, I invite you to envision the vibrant tapestry of colors, flavors, and aromas that will grace your raised beds. Picture yourself basking in the pride and joy of cultivating a garden that sustains you and your loved ones. These are the rewards that raised bed gardening bestows upon us—a harmonious fusion of sustenance and a profound connection with the natural world.

WHAT EXACTLY IS RAISED BED GARDENING?

One gardening method that I find genuinely fascinating is raised bed gardening. To build an elevated growing space in our own backyard, it involves the use of structures that are installed on top of the existing soil. The steps involved in raised bed gardening are as follows:

1. **Calculate the size:** Choosing the raised bed's dimensions is the first step in raised bed gardening. Think about the plants you wish to grow and the

space you have in your yard. The elevated bed's length and width can be altered to meet your needs.

2. **Decide on the height:** Determine the raised bed's height. Your level of comfort and gardening choices will determine this. Some favor taller beds that eliminate the need to stoop or kneel, while other people prefer lower beds.

3. **Select the materials:** Choose the materials for your raised bed. Common options include wood, metal, or composite materials. Regarding cost, durability, and aesthetic appeal, each material has advantages of its own.

4. **Build the structure:** Construct the raised bed according to your chosen dimensions and materials. Follow the appropriate construction techniques to ensure stability and longevity.

5. **Prepare the soil:** Put a combination of premium soil, compost, and organic debris in the raised bed. Your plants will benefit from a fertile growing environment as a result. Include materials like gravel or sand at the base of the bed to ensure good drainage.

6. **Plant your crops:** The time has come to plant the chosen crops in the raised bed. Place the plants in the bed, taking into account the unique needs of each one.

7. **Provide regular care:** Raised beds need routine upkeep and care just like any other garden. Provide

the proper fertilization, keep an eye out for pests and illnesses, and water your plants as necessary. Your raised bed garden will also require routine weeding and pruning to stay healthy.

By following these steps, you can establish a thriving raised bed garden that maximizes space, enhances plant growth, and simplifies gardening tasks.

THE ADVANTAGES OF RAISED BED GARDENING

Raised bed gardening offers a multitude of benefits that make it a popular choice for both experienced and novice gardeners alike. Now that my father is in his eighties, he prefers to bring his garden up to his level! Let's explore each of these advantages:

1. **It's better for the soil:** Raised beds provide an opportunity to create a customized soil mix, incorporating the ideal blend of organic matter, compost, and nutrients. This results in a well-drained and fertile soil that promotes healthy plant growth and maximizes yields.
2. **No stooping low:** One of the most appreciated benefits of raised bed gardening is the reduced strain on your back and knees. By elevating the garden, you can comfortably tend to your plants without the need for constant bending or kneeling. This

advantage is especially valuable for individuals with mobility issues or older gardeners who may find traditional gardening methods physically challenging.

3. **They look nice:** In addition to their functional benefits, raised beds also enhance the aesthetics of your garden. The structured and well-defined design adds a visually appealing element, creating an organized and attractive landscape. Whether you opt for rustic wooden beds or sleek metal structures, raised beds can elevate the overall look of your outdoor space.

4. **It's harder for pests to get at plants:** Raised beds provide a natural barrier against pests and critters that may otherwise damage your precious plants. The elevated structure makes it more challenging for ground-dwelling pests, such as slugs or snails, to reach your crops. Additionally, installing protective mesh or fencing around the raised beds further deters unwanted visitors.

5. **Better drainage:** Raised beds also benefit from greater drainage capacities. Waterlogging and the resulting issues of root rot and fungus illnesses are avoided by the simple ability of excess water to flow away. This is especially advantageous in regions with a lot of rainfall or arid soil.

6. **Fewer weeds:** Raised beds offer better weed control compared to traditional gardens. The defined

borders and elevated structure make it easier to spot and remove weeds, reducing competition for nutrients and minimizing the need for excessive weeding.

7. **Longer growing seasons:** Raised beds warm up faster in the spring, allowing for an extended growing season. The elevated soil absorbs and retains heat more efficiently, providing a favorable environment for early planting and encouraging plant growth. Additionally, the improved drainage helps prevent waterlogged soil, which can hinder root development and limit growth.

8. **They are good for beginner gardeners:** Raised beds are an excellent choice for novice gardeners, as they provide a controlled and manageable gardening space. The smaller size and contained environment make it easier to learn the basics of gardening, such as soil preparation, watering, and plant care.

Raised bed gardening encompasses an array of advantages that enhance the overall gardening experience. From improving soil quality and reducing physical strain to creating visually appealing gardens and providing a host of pest and weed control benefits, raised beds offer a practical and rewarding approach to growing plants. Thinking about raised beds can alter your gardening experience, whether you're an experienced gardener or just getting started.

TYPES OF RAISED BEDS

It's time to choose the perfect raised bed for your garden! In this section, we will go over the three main types of raised beds and the various materials commonly used to construct them.

Raised Ground Beds: Raised ground beds are the simplest form of raised beds, consisting of additional soil added to the existing ground level. These beds have no supporting structure and are ideal for gardeners looking for a cost-effective and straightforward solution. Raised ground beds offer improved soil drainage and aeration, along with easier access for planting, weeding, and harvesting.

Steps to create raised ground beds:

1. Select the desired location for your raised garden bed.
2. Clear the area of any weeds or debris.
3. Begin adding soil to the designated area, gradually building up to the desired height.
4. Level the soil surface, ensuring it is evenly distributed.
5. Plant your desired crops or plants in the raised ground bed.

Supported Raised Beds: Supported raised beds are similar to raised ground beds but feature a structural support system around the edges such as wood, untreated lumber, natural stone, bricks, metal, or plastic. The support structure provides stability to the raised bed, prevents soil erosion, and adds an aesthetic element to your garden.

Steps to Create Supported Raised Beds:

1. Choose the desired material for the supporting structure of your raised bed.
2. Determine the size and shape of your raised bed and mark the boundaries.
3. Clear the area and level the ground.
4. Assemble the supporting structure by connecting the chosen materials securely.
5. Fill the raised bed with quality soil, leaving sufficient space for plant roots.
6. Plant your preferred crops or plants, ensuring appropriate spacing and depth.

Containerized Raised Beds: Containerized raised beds are larger, self-contained structures that are perfect for gardeners with limited space or those looking for a more portable option. These beds can be made from various materials, including wood, plastic, or metal. Containerized raised beds offer flexibility, allowing you to position your garden anywhere you desire, such as on patios, balconies, or rooftops.

Steps to Create Containerized Raised Beds:

1. Select a suitable container for your raised bed, ensuring it has adequate drainage holes.
2. Place the container in the desired location, ensuring it receives sufficient sunlight.
3. Fill the container with high-quality soil, leaving enough space for plant roots to grow.
4. Plant your chosen crops or plants, considering their specific spacing and watering requirements.
5. Water the plants regularly, ensuring the containerized raised bed retains proper moisture levels.

Now that we have explored the different types of raised beds, let's take a closer look at the materials commonly used to construct them:

- **Wood and untreated lumber:** Wood and untreated lumber are popular choices for raised beds due to their natural aesthetics and accessibility. Redwood and cedar are great options since they are inherently resistant to decay and insect invasion. However, untreated lumber may degrade over time, requiring periodic maintenance or replacement.
- **Natural stone:** Natural stone offers a durable and long-lasting option for raised beds. Stones such as limestone, granite, or sandstone provide a rustic and

charming look. They ensure a healthy growing environment for your plants by providing appropriate drainage and heat retention.

- **Bricks:** Bricks are a classic choice for constructing raised beds. They offer stability, durability, and timeless appeal. Ensure the bricks are stacked tightly, leaving no gaps for soil to escape.
- **Metal:** Metal raised beds, typically made of galvanized steel or aluminum, offer strength and durability. They are a low-maintenance choice because they are resistant to decay, pests, and weathering. Metal beds are simple to modify to your preferred specifications.
- **Plastic:** Plastic raised beds are lightweight, affordable, and easy to assemble. They are resistant to rot and provide good insulation for plant roots. However, ensure the plastic used is food-safe if you plan to grow edible crops.

Remember to choose materials that align with your budget, your aesthetic preferences, and the specific needs of your plants.

PLANNING FOR YOUR RAISED BEDS

Before you move into the actual construction and planting, it is crucial to plan the location of your raised beds carefully. In this section, we will guide you through the process of selecting the ideal location for your raised beds, taking into consideration factors such as sunlight exposure, protection from the elements, proximity to water, and accessibility.

1. **Assess sunlight exposure:** The amount of sunlight your raised beds receive is a vital consideration for successful plant growth. Determine whether your chosen area receives full sun (at least 6 hours of direct sunlight), part sun (3 to 6 hours of sunlight), or part shade (3 to 6 hours of sunlight with some protection from harsh sunlight). This information will help you select plants that are well suited to your garden's lighting conditions.

2. **Evaluate south-facing locations:** The south side of your garden is often the best place for raised beds. South-facing locations receive ample sunlight throughout the day, providing optimal growing conditions for a wide range of plants. Additionally, placing your raised beds near a tall structure, such as a fence or wall, can offer protection from strong winds and other elements that may impact plant health.

3. **Consider proximity to water:** Another essential factor to consider when planning the location of your raised beds is their proximity to a water source. It is important to choose a location that is convenient for watering your plants. Placing your raised beds closer to a water supply, such as an

outdoor faucet or rainwater collection system, will make it easier to provide the necessary moisture to your plants, especially during hot and dry periods.

4. **Ensure accessibility to the home:** If you are growing your own food in raised beds, it is beneficial to position them closer to your home. This proximity ensures easy access for harvesting fresh produce, tending plants, and monitoring their progress. Having your raised beds within reach of the kitchen can make the entire gardening experience more enjoyable and convenient.

5. **Evaluate soil quality:** Before finalizing the location, consider the quality of the soil in the chosen area. Raised beds offer the advantage of creating a controlled environment with improved soil conditions. However, it is still essential to assess the soil's drainage, nutrient content, and structure. If necessary, soil amendments can be incorporated to optimize growing conditions.

6. **Observe potential obstructions:** Take a walk around the chosen area and observe any potential obstructions that may affect the growth of your plants. Consider factors such as overhanging trees or structures that may cast unwanted shade, compete for nutrients, or hinder airflow. It is best to select a location with minimal obstructions to ensure the health and vitality of your raised bed plants.

7. **Plan for expansion:** If you have the space, consider planning for future expansion of your raised bed garden. Leave adequate room between each raised bed to allow for easy movement, maintenance, and potential expansion in the future. Proper spacing will also facilitate proper airflow and prevent overcrowding of plants.

By following these steps and carefully considering sunlight exposure, protection from the elements, proximity to water, accessibility, soil quality, and potential obstructions, you can select the perfect location for your raised beds.

Interactive Element

Now that we are armed with knowledge about the different types of raised beds and their advantages, it's time to roll up our sleeves and dig into the practical aspects of creating our own raised beds. But before we do, let's take a moment to reflect on the planning process and how it has prepared us for this exciting endeavor.

Planning is the backbone of any successful garden, and raised bed gardening is no exception. As we've learned, considering factors such as sunlight exposure, location, and proximity to water can greatly influence the productivity and convenience of our raised beds. Armed with this understanding, we can now take a step further and visualize our garden layout using some paper and a writing utensil. Blank paper or graph paper serves as our canvas, allowing us to sketch a plan that incorporates the knowledge gained throughout this chapter. It's like creating a blueprint for our dream garden, tailored to our specific needs and preferences. This hands-on approach not only deepens our understanding but also empowers us to bring our vision to life.

Now, with our garden plan in hand, we're ready to transition into the practical aspects of creating raised beds. It's an exciting phase that requires a few essential tools and materials. Assembling the necessary equipment beforehand ensures a smooth and efficient process. We'll need basic tools like a shovel, rake, and hand trowel to prepare the ground and loosen the soil. Depending on the material chosen for our raised beds, we may also require a saw or drill for cutting and fastening. While wood is a popular choice, options like natural stone, bricks, metal, and plastic offer their own unique benefits and aesthetics. Choosing the right material aligns with our garden's overall design and ensures durability. In my yard, I have raised beds made from cedar that my husband built. I also have a kit that we bought from a local garden store that is made of galvanized steel. I have another location in our yard where we used leftover landscape blocks to put in a partial frame that butts up to the galvanized steel raised bed.

We also need to think about the soil and additives in addition to the materials. We can have more control over the soil composition by using raised beds. To increase its richness and structure, we can enrich it with organic material, like old manure or compost. Healthy plant growth and substantial yields are enabled by proper soil preparation.

2

TOOLS AND EQUIPMENT YOU WILL NEED

Confucius once wisely said, "A workman who wants to do his work well must first prepare his tools." This ancient wisdom holds true even in the realm of gardening. Before you start building productive raised beds, it is essential to have the right tools and equipment. In this chapter, we will discuss gardening tools and ensure we have everything we need to bring our vision to life.

To build our raised beds successfully, we'll need a variety of tools, each serving a specific purpose. The basic tools include a sturdy shovel, a rake, and a hand trowel. These workhorses are indispensable when it comes to preparing the ground and loosening the soil. With their assistance, we can create a suitable foundation for our raised beds and ensure proper drainage.

Depending on the materials we choose for our raised beds, additional tools might be necessary. For instance, if we opt for wooden beds, having a saw or drill will enable us to cut and fasten the lumber with precision. On the other hand, if we decide to explore alternatives like metal or plastic, we may require specific tools to handle these materials effectively. By understanding the requirements of our chosen materials, we can equip ourselves accordingly and execute our plans with confidence.

In our quest for resourcefulness and sustainability, we'll also explore the concept of upcycling. It's fascinating how everyday objects can be repurposed to create unique and eye-catching raised beds. By thinking outside the box and breathing new life into old items, we not only minimize waste but also infuse our gardens with a touch of creativity and individuality. So, keep an open mind as we discover innovative ways to repurpose materials and turn them into beautiful, functional raised beds.

As we progress through this chapter, we will strive to provide step-by-step guides for building raised beds using different materials, ensuring that you have a comprehensive resource at your disposal.

THE SIMPLEST RAISED BED GARDEN DESIGN

We will now go through the most practical designs for a raised bed garden. This design will provide us with a 4 x 6-

foot raised bed, standing at a height of 24 inches. This design provides ample space for deep-rooted vegetables and even miniature fruit trees. Follow these steps and guidelines to bring your raised bed garden to life.

Step 1: Gather materials to build your raised bed. You will need the following materials:

- Untreated wood boards (preferably cedar or redwood) for the bedframe
- Galvanized screws or nails for assembly
- Linseed or tung oil (optional) for wood treatment
- Fine wire mesh or hard cloth (optional) for rodent protection

Step 2: Determine the bed size. For this design, we will create a rectangular bed measuring 4 by 6 feet. This size offers a good balance between space and manageability. To suit your particular demands and fit your available space, feel free to modify the dimensions.

Step 3: Construct the bedframe. Using the untreated wood boards, assemble the bedframe. Place the longer boards (6-foot) on the sides and the shorter boards (4-foot) at the ends. Secure the corners with galvanized screws or nails, ensuring a sturdy and stable structure.

Step 4: Treat the wood (optional). To increase the durability and longevity of the wood, you can treat it with linseed or tung oil. The outer surfaces of the bedframe should be coated with a thin layer of the selected oil. Before continuing, let the oil totally dry out.

Step 5: Reinforce the corners. For added strength and stability, consider reinforcing the corners of the raised bed. This can be done by attaching metal L-brackets or corner braces to each corner, both inside and outside of the bedframe. This will prevent the corners from shifting or weakening over time. You can also use ground stakes nailed to each corner and in the middle. This is how my husband builds them in our yard.

Step 6: Add wire mesh or hard cloth (optional). If you anticipate problems with digging rodents, such as moles or gophers, it's wise to add a layer of protection to the bottom of your raised bed. Cut a piece of fine wire mesh or hard cloth to fit the dimensions of the bedframe. Before adding soil, secure it to the base of the bedframe. This barrier will help prevent rodents from accessing the bed from below.

Step 7: Prepare the location. Choose a suitable location for your raised bed, ensuring it receives adequate sunlight for the plants you intend to grow. Make a clean, level surface for the bed by clearing the area of any weeds or waste.

Step 8: Place the raised bed. The raised bed should be moved to the desired spot. By running a spirit level across the top of the bed frame, you can make sure it is level. Adjust the position if necessary.

Step 9: Fill the bed with soil. A good-quality gardening soil mixture should be used to fill the raised bed. Aim for a mix that is well-draining, nutrient-rich, and suitable for the plants you plan to grow. You can buy soil that has already been blended or make your own by adding topsoil, compost, and other organic additives.

Step 10: Plant and care for your garden. Now that your raised bed is complete and filled with soil, it's time to plant your favorite vegetables, herbs, or even miniature fruit trees. Follow proper planting guidelines, including spacing, watering, and maintenance practices, to ensure the success of your garden.

By following these steps and incorporating the optional measures of reinforcing corners and adding wire mesh or hard cloth for rodent protection, you can create a simple yet effective raised bed garden design. This design offers ample space for a variety of plants while ensuring the longevity and stability of the bed structure.

Here is a raised bed my husband made and used ground stakes to reinforce corners and middle.

Outside corner

Inside corner

*Another raised bed in our yard. The dimensions are 4' x 8'.
This raised bed holds a crop of carrots, beets, radishes,
pepperoncini peppers, lettuce, basil and tomatoes.*

STONE RAISED BEDS

Stone raised beds are a true testament to the artistry and craftsmanship of gardening, offering both aesthetic appeal and practicality. In this section, we will explore the difference between dry stacking and using landscaping glue to hold the stones in place and provide you with a comprehensive step-by-step guide to building your own stone garden bed.

Understanding Dry Stacking vs. Using Landscaping Glue

Dry stacking and using landscaping glue are two common methods for constructing stone raised beds. Each approach has its advantages and disadvantages, and it's important to choose the one that aligns with your preferences and the desired outcome.

Dry Stacking: Dry stacking involves carefully selecting and arranging stones without the use of any adhesive. This method offers a more natural and rustic look, allowing the stones to interlock and create a stable structure. It provides flexibility and allows for easy modifications or disassembly if needed. Dry stacking also promotes better drainage as it allows water to flow freely between the stones.

Using Landscaping Glue: Alternatively, using landscaping glue involves applying a suitable adhesive between the stones to hold them firmly in place. This method provides a more permanent and secure structure, ensuring that the stones remain in position even under heavy pressure or movement. High wind or foot traffic regions are perfect for it. However, it may limit the flexibility for modifications or disassembly in the future.

Below is a step-by-step guide for building your stone garden bed:

Step 1: Planning and Design. Determine the size, shape, and location of your stone raised bed. Think about things like the amount of space you have, the amount of sunlight, and accessibility. Sketch a layout to visualize the design and estimate the quantity of stones required.

Step 2: Gather Materials and Tools. Collect the following materials and tools:

- Stones of your choice (varying sizes and shapes)
- Gravel or crushed stone (for the base)
- Landscaping fabric or any other barrier (optional, for weed control)
- Shovel or garden trowel
- Level
- Rubber mallet or hammer
- Landscaping glue (if using this method)
- Safety goggles and gloves (recommended)

Step 3: Prepare the Site. The area where the raised stone bed will be built should be cleared. Get rid of any existing plants, rocks, or garbage. Make sure the ground is level and devoid of any obstructions that can affect the stability of the building.

Step 4: Create a Base. If desired, lay a layer of landscaping fabric over the prepared ground to prevent weed growth. This step is optional but can help maintain a clean and tidy appearance. Next, spread a layer of gravel or crushed stone evenly across the bed area. This will provide a stable foundation and aid in drainage.

Step 5: Start Stacking Stones. Begin by selecting your largest and most uniform stones for the base layer. Place them along the perimeter of the bed, ensuring they are level and snugly fit together. Verify the stones' vertical and horizontal alignment with a level.

Step 6: Continue Building Layers. Add subsequent layers of stones, staggering them to create stability and strength. Fit the stones tightly together, interlocking them as much as possible. For dry stacking, avoid excessive gaps between stones. If using landscaping glue, apply it sparingly and according to the manufacturer's instructions.

Step 7: Check for Levelness and Stability. Periodically use a level to ensure that the stones are level both horizontally and vertically. Adjust the stones as needed to maintain stability and balance. Tap gently with a rubber mallet or hammer to secure them in place.

Step 8: Complete the Bed. Keep piling stones until your raised bed is the right height. Remember to maintain proper alignment and stability throughout the process. For a finishing touch, cap the top layer with flat stones to create a neat and polished appearance.

Step 9: Optional Steps. If using dry stacking, consider filling the gaps between the stones with soil or gravel to prevent weed growth and improve the overall aesthetics. If using landscaping glue, allow sufficient drying time as recommended by the product instructions before proceeding with filling the raised bed.

Step 10: Fill and Plant. Add a quality garden soil mix to the raised bed, leaving adequate space for planting. Select suitable plants and flowers based on your gardening preferences and the growing conditions provided by the raised bed.

This is also in our backyard; these flat stones were left over from another project. They are stacked on top of each other with no adhesive.

METAL RAISED BEDS

Raised beds can be made from a variety of materials, each of which has advantages and things to consider. While wooden beds are a popular choice, metal raised beds offer a durable and long-lasting alternative. In this section, we will explore the benefits of metal beds and provide a step-by-step guide to making a galvanized steel bed.

Metal beds require more effort during the construction process, but their longevity makes them a worthwhile investment. Unlike wooden beds that may deteriorate over time due to exposure to moisture, pests, and rot, metal beds can withstand the elements and provide a sturdy framework for your garden.

To make a galvanized steel bed, follow these step-by-step instructions:

1. Measure and cut the galvanized steel sheets according to the desired dimensions of your raised bed. Remember that accuracy is essential in this situation, so take your time and confirm your measurements.
2. Once your sheets are cut, assemble the bed by attaching the corner brackets to the steel sheets. To provide the bed with solidity and strength, make sure the brackets are well secured.

3. Now it's time to secure the steel sheets together. Position the sheets in the desired configuration, making sure they are aligned correctly. Use the self-tapping screws and a drill to connect the sheets, ensuring a tight and secure fit.

4. After assembling the main structure, check the levelness of the bed. It's essential to do this to guarantee appropriate drainage and avoid water accumulating in particular places. Adjust the bed as needed until it is perfectly level.

5. Once you are satisfied with the levelness of your metal raised bed, it's time to prepare the site for installation. Make sure the ground is level and thoroughly compacted and remove any grass or weeds from the area.

6. Finally, place your metal raised bed in its designated spot. Make sure it is stable and not swaying from the ground. Now, it's time to fill it with nutrient-rich soil and start planting your favorite vegetables, herbs, or flowers.

You have now successfully built your own metal raised bed. Now sit back, unwind, and watch your plants flourish in their chic, long-lasting habitat.

ARE RAISED BED KITS WORTH IT?

When considering whether raised bed kits are worth the investment, it ultimately comes down to personal preferences and circumstances. Factors such as the availability of materials, time constraints, and desired aesthetics can all influence the decision. In this section, we will explore the different types of raised bed kits available and provide a rough guide to their prices, empowering readers to make an informed choice.

There are various types of raised bed kits available on the market, each with its own advantages and considerations. Let's take a closer look at some popular options:

1. **Wooden kits:** Wooden raised bed kits are a classic choice, providing a natural and rustic look to the garden. These kits are usually made from durable and rot-resistant wood, such as cedar or pine. Prices for wooden kits can vary depending on the size and design, ranging from around $50 for a small basic kit to several hundred dollars for larger or more intricate designs.

2. **Metal kits:** Metal raised bed kits offer a modern and sleek aesthetic. They are often constructed from galvanized steel or aluminum, which provides durability and longevity. These kits may come in modular designs that allow for expansion or customization. Prices for metal kits can vary

significantly, starting from around $80 for a basic kit and going up to several hundred dollars for larger or specialized options.

3. **Composite kits:** Composite raised bed kits are made from a blend of wood fibers and recycled plastics, offering the durability of plastic and the natural appearance of wood. These kits are an eco-conscious choice and typically fall within the price range of wooden kits.

4. **Elevated kits:** Elevated raised bed kits are designed to be at a comfortable height for gardening, eliminating the need for bending or kneeling. These kits often feature a combination of wood and metal and come with built-in legs or stands. Prices for elevated kits can range from around $100 to $300 or more, depending on the size and features.

This was a raised bed kit we purchased on sale at a local garden center. It's made from galvanized steel and each side is about 40". Purchase price was approximately $39.99.

While raised bed kits may come at a higher upfront cost compared to building your own beds, they offer convenience and a streamlined assembly process. Additionally, they often include warranties, ensuring peace of mind in terms of product quality and longevity.

RAISED BEDS THE UPCYCLED WAY

Let's dive in and explore how recycled raised beds can inspire creativity, cut costs, and elevate your garden to the next level.

When it comes to upcycled raised beds, the sky's the limit. Seriously, anything with sufficient depth can be repurposed into a fantastic gardening haven. Imagine transforming an old bathtub into a blooming oasis or turning a water trough into a thriving vegetable patch. The possibilities are endless, and the results are truly awe-inspiring.

Here's a gem I stumbled upon, an old bookshelf as a raised bed. I kid you not! Picture this—a bookshelf filled with lush greens and colorful flowers, becoming a living work of art right in your garden. It's not just practical; it's an upcycling masterpiece that will have people you know scratching their heads in amazement. Talk about turning a new leaf— quite literally!

But that's not all, we're just scratching the surface of upcycled raised beds. Get this—sinks, old paddling pools, and even plastic bottles can join the gardening party. Yes, you heard me right! Sinks can be transformed into delightful herb gardens, adding a touch of whimsy and practicality to your outdoor space. And let's not forget about the old paddling pool—the perfect canvas for your vegetable dreams to come to life. It's like having your own mini-farm, complete with a splash of nostalgia.

Now, brace yourselves for a truly "green" idea—raised beds made from plastic bottles. Just envision a colorful mosaic of bottles, filled with soil and sprouting greenery. It's a sight that will make Mother Nature herself give you a standing ovation. Additionally, it's a great way to use those plastic bottles and lessen waste. Who said gardening couldn't be witty and sustainable at the same time?

Let's talk about the sheer brilliance of upcycled raised beds. Not only do they breathe new life into forgotten objects, but they also inject personality and charm into your garden. Imagine the joy of harvesting fresh vegetables from an old bathtub or admiring a blooming flowerbed in an upcycled sink. It's like giving these items a second chance at greatness, all while creating a one-of-a-kind oasis that reflects your unique style.

But here's the icing on the cake—upcycled raised beds are a budget-friendly alternative that will leave your wallet singing with joy. By repurposing materials that would otherwise end up in the landfill, you're not only saving money but also making a positive impact on the environment. It's a win-win situation that will make you feel like the gardening superhero you were always meant to be.

TOOLS YOU NEED FOR RAISED BED GARDENING

Raised bed gardening requires a few essential tools to ensure successful cultivation and maintenance of your garden. In this section, we will explore the tools that are invaluable for tending to your raised beds and helping your plants thrive.

- **Gloves:** The best gardening gloves are crucial for shielding your hands from soil-borne infections, sharp edges, and thorns. Choose gloves that are durable, breathable, and provide a snug fit to ensure comfort and dexterity while working in the garden.

- **Pruning Shears:** Secateurs, commonly referred to as pruning shears, are crucial for preserving the health and form of your plants. They are perfect for pruning branches, cutting flower stems that have become infected, and removing harmed or damaged plant sections. Look for shears with a sharp, bypass-style blade that can slice through stems cleanly.
- **Fork:** A sturdy garden fork is useful for turning the soil, loosening compacted areas, and incorporating amendments or compost into the raised beds. It helps improve soil aeration and drainage, promoting healthy root growth.
- **Trowel:** A trowel is a handheld tool with a narrow, scoop-shaped blade that is perfect for digging small holes, transplanting seedlings, and planting bulbs or annuals. Choose a trowel with a comfortable handle and a strong, rust-resistant blade.
- **Spade:** A spade is a larger version of a trowel and is essential for heavier-duty digging tasks. It is useful for digging large planting holes, edging beds, and moving soil or compost. A spade with a strong handle and a long-lasting, sharp blade is what you want.
- **Hoe:** A garden hoe is beneficial for weeding and cultivating the soil around your raised beds. It helps remove weeds and break up compacted soil, preventing competition for nutrients and improving water penetration.

- **Garden Scissors:** Garden scissors, also known as pruning scissors or snips, are versatile tools for precise pruning, deadheading, and harvesting. They are particularly useful for delicate or small-scale tasks, such as trimming herbs or harvesting flowers.

You'll be well-prepared to handle the numerous duties involved in raised bed gardening if you arm yourself with the necessary equipment.

Interactive Element

Here are the key items you will need to kickstart your raised bed journey:

1. **Raised Bed Materials:** Whether you opt for wood, metal, or another sturdy material, make sure it suits your style and budget. Remember, durability is key, as we want our raised beds to withstand the test of time and weather.
2. **Soil:** The foundation of your garden kingdom! Nothing is more crucial than getting the quality of your soil right from the beginning. The soil will be your plants' main source of nutrition, their lifeblood. So, be sure to invest in nutrient-rich soil, teeming with organic matter, ready to nourish your green darlings. It's like serving them a five-star meal every day!

3. **Compost:** Ah, the magic ingredient that turns average soil into a superhero blend. Compost is a gardener's secret weapon, brimming with nutrients and beneficial microorganisms. Adding compost to your raised beds is like sprinkling fairy dust—it transforms your garden into a thriving ecosystem, bursting with life and vitality.

4. **Seeds or Seedlings:** What's a garden without its stars —the plants themselves? Choose your favorite vegetables, herbs, or flowers, and let the planting extravaganza begin. Whether you prefer starting from seeds or opt for ready-to-plant seedlings, the choice is yours. Just make sure to select varieties suited to your climate and growing conditions.

5. **Watering Can or Hose:** Our plants need hydration, just like we do. So, let's arm ourselves with a trusty watering can or hose to quench their thirst. It's a delightful ritual, a moment of connection with our green companions. Plus, who doesn't love a bit of splashing around with water?

With these essentials in hand, you are one step closer to getting started on building raised beds!

In the next chapter, we'll dig deep into the topic of soil preparation and amendments. We'll uncover the mysteries of pH levels, discuss the magic of organic fertilizers, and unleash the power of beneficial microorganisms. Together, we'll cultivate a garden that's not just visually stunning but also a haven for flourishing plant life.

3

PREPARING RAISED BEDS WITH A SPRINKLE OF SOIL SCIENCE

Ready to unlock the foundation for a healthy garden? This chapter explains how soil science makes all the difference in your gardening success. Understanding the characteristics of healthy soil, conducting soil tests, and making necessary adjustments are essential steps in creating optimal conditions for your raised beds. We will also explore the importance of mulching and the benefits of no-till gardening techniques. Lastly, we will guide you on how to create your own compost, a valuable source of nutrients for your plants.

The main focus of this chapter is to equip you with the knowledge and tools to cultivate healthy soil in your raised beds. By understanding the composition of the soil and its impact on plant growth, you can make informed decisions to enhance productivity and sustainability in your garden.

Soil is a valuable resource. Human activity is contributing to the destruction and depletion of soil which takes thousands of years to develop. Disturbingly, current estimates suggest that there is only enough topsoil remaining to sustain us for the next 60 years. The urgency to protect and nurture our soil has never been greater. In this chapter, we will discuss the importance of soil conservation and offer practical insights to help you contribute to the preservation of this valuable resource.

WHAT NUTRIENTS DO PLANTS TAKE FROM SOIL?

Have you ever wondered what exactly plants need from the soil to thrive and grow? This section covers the essential nutrients plants require for their health and vitality. We will uncover the benefits of nitrogen, phosphorus, potassium, calcium, magnesium, sulfur, and of course, trace elements as well!

Start with the three main elements: nitrogen, phosphorus, and potassium, also known as NPK. These major elements play pivotal roles in a plant's growth and development. Nitrogen is like fuel for plants, driving their leafy green growth and providing the necessary building blocks for proteins, enzymes, and chlorophyll. On the other hand, phosphorus is in charge of transferring energy within the plant. It aids in processes such as photosynthesis, root development, and the formation of flowers and fruits. Finally, potassium acts as a guardian, strengthening plants against diseases, regulating water usage, and promoting overall plant vigor.

While NPK steals much of the spotlight, other major elements also deserve our attention. Calcium, for instance, plays a crucial role in cell wall structure, ensuring sturdy plant architecture. It also aids in the transportation of other nutrients within the plant, facilitating their efficient uptake. Magnesium is another essential player, as it forms a vital component of chlorophyll, the pigment that allows plants to harness the energy of sunlight. Additionally, magnesium influences the activation of enzymes involved in various metabolic processes. Lastly, sulfur contributes to the formation of proteins and vitamins, promoting healthy plant growth and playing a part in the synthesis of essential compounds.

Beyond the major elements, there is a world of trace elements that, despite being required in minute quantities, are equally important for plant growth. These include iron, zinc, manganese, copper, molybdenum, and boron, among others. Each trace element has its own unique function within the plant, be it in enzyme activation, hormone synthesis, or electron transport. While they may be needed in small doses, their absence or deficiency can have significant consequences for plant health and productivity.

It's important to note that plant nutrient requirements can vary depending on plant species, soil conditions, and environmental factors. The secret to giving your plants the ideal nutritional balance is to understand their unique requirements as well as those of the soil in which they are grown. Soil testing and analysis can be invaluable in determining nutrient levels and any potential deficiencies, helping you make informed decisions when it comes to fertilization and soil amendments.

HOW TO PREPARE GARDEN SOIL FOR RAISED BEDS

Are you ready to transform your garden soil into the perfect growing medium for your raised beds? In this section, we'll go over how to get your garden soil ready for the best texture, drainage, and pH levels. Let's start now.

Step 1: Assess Your Garden Soil. Take a close look at your existing garden soil. Note its texture, drainage, and pH levels. Remember, compact soil with poor drainage and inappropriate pH may not be suitable for raised beds.

Step 2: Gather Materials. Collect the following materials:

- Garden fork or shovel
- Compost or fresh potting soil
- Organic matter (compost, well-rotted manure, or leaf mold)
- pH testing kit or DIY soil testing materials (vinegar and baking soda)
- Watering can or hose

Step 3: Make Room for It. Remove all weeds, rocks, and other obstructions from the area where you intend to build your raised beds. This will provide a clean and even surface for your new soil.

Step 4: Loosen the Soil. Using a garden fork or shovel, loosen the garden soil to improve aeration and break up any compacted areas. This will allow for better root penetration and drainage.

Step 5: Test the Soil pH. Perform a soil pH test using a testing kit or the DIY method. Follow the instructions provided to obtain an accurate reading. Determine if the pH falls within the desired range of 5.8 to 7.5. If it doesn't, adjustments will be necessary.

Step 6: Adjust the pH. To increase pH (make soil more alkaline), add small amounts of baking soda to the soil and mix thoroughly. Include organic matter in the soil, such as compost or well-rotted manure, to lower pH (make the soil more acidic). To confirm that the desired pH range is reached following changes, perform the pH test again.

Step 7: Improve Soil Texture. Blend the garden soil with fresh potting soil or compost to enhance its texture. Mix the two types of soil in a ratio of approximately 3 parts garden soil to 1 part potting soil or compost. This combination will provide a balanced medium for your raised beds.

Step 8: Include Organic Material. Add organic material to the soil mixture, such as compost, well-rotted manure, or leaf mold. Improved soil structure, nutrient addition, and moisture retention are all benefits of organic matter. Aim for a percentage of organic matter in the soil that is between 20 and 30 percent.

Step 9: Mix Thoroughly. Using a garden fork or shovel, thoroughly mix the soil, potting soil/compost, and organic matter together. Make sure the ingredients are mixed into the mixture equally.

Step 10: Level the Soil. Rake the soil mixture to create a smooth and level surface in your raised beds. This will create a level planting space and stop water from gathering in specific places.

Step 11: Water the Soil. Use a hose or watering bucket to fully moisten the soil. This will guarantee that the soil settles and that your plants have good initial moisture levels.

Step 12: Leave the Soil to Settle. Prior to planting, give the soil time to settle. This will give time for any air pockets to escape and for the soil components to integrate.

Step 13: Conduct Periodic Soil Tests. As your raised beds progress, it is essential to conduct periodic soil tests to monitor nutrient levels and pH. This will help you make necessary adjustments over time to maintain a healthy growing environment.

You will successfully prepare your garden soil for raised beds if you follow these instructions.

WHAT IS MULCH?

Have you ever wondered about the mysterious layer of material known as mulch and its role in gardening? In this section, we will unravel the secrets of mulch and delve into its various benefits when used in raised beds. Let's explore the reasons behind mulching, the different types of organic mulch available, and the best practices for adding mulch to your raised beds.

Mulch serves as a protective layer that is added to raised beds for multiple reasons. One of its primary purposes is weed prevention. By applying a layer of mulch, such as cardboard placed at the bottom of the bed, you create a barrier that inhibits weed growth. This natural weed control method can save you time and effort spent on frequent weeding, allowing your plants to flourish without competition from unwanted plants.

Mulch's capacity to keep soil moist is another advantage. By covering the surface of the raised bed with a layer of mulch, you create a barrier that reduces evaporation, thus helping to conserve water. This is particularly crucial in hot, dry settings or during droughts. Consistent moisture levels in the soil promote healthy plant growth and reduce the frequency of watering.

Mulch can help protect plants from wintertime frost damage. A layer of organic mulch, such as straw or wood chips, acts as insulation, protecting the plant roots from extreme temperature fluctuations. This is particularly beneficial for perennial plants that remain in the raised bed year-round.

Mulch has many benefits for the soil, including weed control, moisture retention, and the addition of nutrients as it decomposes. Compost, grass clippings, and shredded leaves are examples of organic mulches that progressively decay and release nutrients into the soil. This natural process enriches the soil, providing a steady supply of essential elements for plant growth.

Now that we understand the benefits of mulch, let's explore the different types of organic mulch available:

1. **Compost:** This nutrient-rich mulch is created from decomposed organic matter, such as kitchen scraps, yard waste, and plant materials. It increases moisture retention, increases soil fertility, and offers a slow-release source of nutrients.

2. **Straw:** Commonly found in vegetable gardens is straw mulch. It aids with weed control, moisture retention, and protection from temperature extremes. Hay shouldn't be used, as it can contain weed seeds.

3. **Wood Chips:** Wood chips are popular for their durability and aesthetic appeal. They provide excellent weed control, retain moisture, and gradually break down to enrich the soil. Use aged wood chips to prevent nitrogen depletion.

4. **Shredded Leaves:** Fallen leaves make an excellent mulch option. Shredding them makes them more quickly decomposable, which enhances soil structure, moisture retention, and nutrient availability.

5. **Grass Clippings:** Fresh grass cuttings can be utilized as mulch, yet they must be spread thinly to avoid matting and allow for airflow. They break down and release nitrogen into the soil as they do so.

Now that we have explored the benefits and types of organic mulch, let's discuss when and how to add mulch to your raised beds:

1. **Prepare the Bed:** Before adding mulch, ensure that your raised bed is free of weeds and debris. Level the soil surface and water the bed if necessary.
2. **Select the Best Mulch:** When choosing mulch, consider your plants' individual requirements as well as the local climate. Choose a type that suits your preferences and aligns with the benefits you wish to achieve.
3. **Apply the Mulch:** Spread a layer of mulch evenly over the surface of the raised bed. Aim for a thickness of 2 to 4 inches, taking care not to pile it against the plant stems or tree trunks.
4. **Maintain Mulch Depth:** Monitor the mulch depth over time, as it may settle or decompose. To keep the proper thickness, apply more mulch, as necessary.
5. **Mulch Maintenance:** Periodically check the mulch for weed growth. Any weeds that make it through the mulch layer should be pulled out. Additionally, monitor moisture levels and water the bed as necessary, ensuring that the mulch retains its moisture-retention properties.

By following these steps and incorporating the appropriate organic mulch into your raised beds, you can create an environment that promotes healthy plant growth, reduces weed competition, conserves moisture, and enhances soil fertility.

HOW TO FEED YOUR SOIL

Are you ready to unlock the secret to healthy, nutrient-rich soil? Look no further than compost's transforming abilities. In this section, we will explore the benefits of compost, provide step-by-step instructions for building a compost bin, and dig into the essential elements of composting, including carbon-to-nitrogen ratios and the importance of air and water. Let's dive in and discover how to feed your soil with the magic of compost!

Compost is a valuable organic material that enriches the soil, improves its structure, and enhances overall plant health. It is a nutrient-rich substance produced by the breakdown of organic matter, including leftover food, yard trash, and plant materials. Composting not only keeps waste out of landfills but also improves soil fertility in a sustainable way.

Let's begin by exploring the benefits of compost:

1. **Nutrient-Rich:** Compost contains a wide range of essential nutrients that plants need for healthy growth. These nutrients include nitrogen, phosphorus, potassium, and a host of micronutrients. You may provide your plants with a natural, balanced source of nutrients by adding compost to your soil.

2. **Soil Structure Improvement:** Compost improves soil structure by enhancing its texture, water-

holding capacity, and drainage. It helps sandy soils retain moisture and nutrients, while it aids heavy clay soils in better drainage and aeration. The addition of compost creates a crumbly and well-structured soil that promotes root development and improves overall plant growth.

3. **Soil Fertility Enhancement:** The development of beneficial soil organisms, such as earthworms and microbes, which sustain a healthy soil environment, is supported by compost. By decomposing organic debris, these organisms provide nutrients that are easily accessible to plants. The presence of these organisms also helps suppress harmful pests and diseases.

Now that we understand the benefits of compost, let's explore how to make your own compost bin using pallets and wire:

Step 1: Gather materials. Collect the following materials:

- Wooden pallets (usually available for free)
- Wire mesh or chicken wire
- Nails or screws
- Hammer or screwdriver
- Wire cutters

Step 2: Choose a Location. Select a suitable location for your compost bin. It should be easily accessible and preferably placed on bare soil to allow for beneficial organisms to enter the compost pile.

Step 3: Build the Bin. Arrange three wooden pallets in a U-shape to create the walls of the compost bin. Secure the pallets together at the corners using nails or screws. Cut the wire mesh or chicken wire to size and attach it to the open side of the bin using staples or wire ties. This will enclose the compost pile while still allowing airflow.

Step 4: Layer Organic Material. Start your compost pile by layering organic materials in a balanced manner. Alternate between "browns" and "greens" to achieve the optimal carbon-to-nitrogen ratio. Browns include dry leaves, straw, and shredded paper, while greens consist of kitchen scraps, grass clippings, and fresh plant materials.

Step 5: Maintain Moisture and Aeration. Ensure that your compost pile remains moist, similar to a wrung-out sponge. Use a garden hose or watering can to add water if needed. Additionally, periodically turn the compost pile with a pitchfork or garden fork to promote aeration and decomposition.

Step 6: Monitor and Adjust. Monitor your compost pile regularly. Depending on variables including temperature, moisture, and the size of the compost pile, the decomposition process could take anywhere from a few months to a year. By including more browns or greens as necessary, the carbon-to-nitrogen ratio can be adjusted.

By following these steps, you can create a cost-effective compost bin using readily available materials, allowing you to convert kitchen scraps and yard waste into nutrient-rich compost for your soil.

You should consider the carbon-to-nitrogen ratio to ensure that your compost decomposes as efficiently as possible. About 25 to 30 parts carbon to 1 part nitrogen is the optimal ratio. Carbon-rich items like dry leaves and shredded paper provide the compost pile structure and vitality. Kitchen scraps and recent grass clippings are nitrogen-rich items that provide proteins and encourage microbial activity.

Remember to give your compost pile enough air and water. Regular pile turning encourages oxygen flow, reducing anaerobic degradation and foul smells. To keep the compost pile moist but not drenched in water, water it as needed.

To assist you in composting, we have created a comprehensive chart outlining the different materials suitable for your compost heap. Please refer to the chart below, which categorizes the materials into three columns: greens, browns, and other materials.

Interactive Element

Composting Chart

Greens	Browns	Other Materials
Fruit and veggie scraps	Dry leaves	Eggshells
Grass clippings	Shredded paper	Fireplace ashes
Fresh garden waste	Straw	Untreated wood
Seaweed	Wood chips	Nut shells
Green plant trimmings	Sawdust	Hair and fur
Coffee grounds	Pine needles	
Tea leaves and bags	Cardboard	

Use this chart as a helpful resource to make composting a breeze!

You are well on your way to becoming a successful gardener if you have access to this helpful resource and the knowledge necessary to address the irrigation issue. Keep reading, as in the next chapter we will explore setting up the ultimate watering system, which will enhance your enjoyment and effectiveness of gardening.

4

SETTING UP THE ULTIMATE WATERING SYSTEM

With the increasing frequency and severity of droughts worldwide, water conservation has become more crucial than ever. According to Theworldcounts.com, unless water use is drastically reduced, severe water shortages will affect the entire planet by 2040. As gardeners, it is our responsibility to ensure our plants receive adequate water without any waste. In this chapter, we will explore the ultimate watering system options, allowing you to choose the best method for your garden while promoting efficiency and precision.

Before diving into watering systems, it's essential to understand the signs of overwatering and underwatering in different plant types. Overwatering can lead to yellowing leaves, wilting, root rot, and fungal growth, while underwatering can cause wilting, dry soil, and stunted growth. By being attentive to these signs, you can proactively address any water-related issues and ensure the health of your plants.

As we face increasing water stress and the need for water conservation, setting up the ultimate watering system in our gardens is of utmost importance. By recognizing the signs of overwatering and underwatering in different plant types and selecting the right watering system, we can conserve water, minimize waste, and promote healthy plant growth. Whether you opt for drip irrigation, soaker hoses, sprinkler systems, or automated timers, choose the method that best suits your garden's needs. Let's strive for efficiency and precision in our watering practices, ensuring the vitality of our plants while contributing to water conservation efforts.

WHAT PLANTS TELL US ABOUT WATER NEEDS

Water is a vital resource for the survival and growth of plants. As gardeners and caretakers, it's crucial for us to understand the signs plants exhibit when they need water or when they are being overwatered. By paying close attention to these indicators, we can ensure that our plants receive the appropriate amount of hydration for optimal health. In this section, we will explore the four signs of overwatering plants and delve into the effects of water stress and drought.

Broccoli leaves after rainfall.

Signs of overwatering

Overwatering can have detrimental effects on plant health. By recognizing these signs, we can take corrective measures to prevent damage. According to BrightView, a leading landscaping services provider, there are four main indicators of overwatering plants:

- **Yellowing Leaves:** Overwatered plants often display yellowing leaves. This occurs because excessive moisture prevents the roots from absorbing necessary nutrients, leading to a nutrient deficiency.

- **Wilting:** Surprisingly, wilting can be a sign of both overwatering and underwatering. Overwatered plants may appear limp and droopy due to the lack of oxygen available to the roots. It is important to differentiate between the two causes by assessing other signs.
- **Root Rot:** Excessive watering can lead to root rot, a condition where the roots become waterlogged, and oxygen-starved. Affected roots may appear brown and mushy. This can inhibit the plant's ability to uptake water and nutrients effectively.
- **Fungus or Mold Growth:** Overwatering creates a favorable environment for the growth of fungi and molds. If you notice fuzzy white or gray patches on the soil surface or on the plant itself, it could indicate excessive moisture.

Water Stress and Drought

While overwatering is a common mistake, it is equally important to recognize the signs of water stress and drought in plants. The Missouri Botanical Garden provides valuable insights into identifying and managing these conditions:

- **Leaf Curling:** During water stress, plants tend to conserve water by curling their leaves. This reduces the leaf surface area exposed to the sun, minimizing water loss through transpiration.

- **Leaf Wilting:** Similar to overwatering, water-stressed plants may exhibit wilting. The leaves lose their turgidity and appear limp. Unlike overwatering, the soil may feel dry to the touch.
- **Leaf Scorch:** As water stress intensifies, plants may display leaf scorching. This occurs when the demand for water exceeds the supply, resulting in the plant's inability to transport sufficient moisture to all its tissues.
- **Stunted Growth:** In times of prolonged water stress or drought, plants may experience reduced growth rates. This is their way of conserving energy and focusing on survival rather than expansion.

Plants serve as excellent indicators of their water needs, displaying visible signs that allow us to intervene and provide appropriate care. By observing the signs of overwatering, such as yellowing leaves, wilting, root rot, and fungus growth, we can adjust our watering practices to avoid these issues. Similarly, understanding the signs of water stress and drought, such as leaf curling, wilting, leaf scorch, and stunted growth, empowers us to take timely action and ensure the vitality of our plants. Remember, water is a precious resource, and by paying attention to what plants tell us, we can conserve it while nurturing thriving and resilient green spaces.

HOW MUCH WATER DO PLANTS REALLY NEED?

Water is a vital element for the health and growth of plants. However, understanding how much water plants truly require can be a challenge. In this section, we will explore the optimal water needs of plants and discover effective methods to determine and meet those requirements. By striking the right balance between watering and drainage, we can ensure our plants thrive in a well-hydrated environment.

Optimal Watering: One Inch per Week

Most plants thrive when provided with approximately one inch of water per week. This measurement serves as a general guideline for gardeners to assess the water needs of their plants. To determine how much water this translates to in individual gardens, using a rain gauge can be incredibly helpful. A rain gauge allows you to measure the amount of rainfall your garden receives and make necessary adjustments to your watering routine.

If you don't have a rain gauge, don't worry! You can use any container that can hold water, such as a simple pot or even a measuring cup. Place the container in your garden during rainfall and note the water level after the event. This will give you an estimate of how much water your plants are receiving naturally and how much additional watering they may require.

Importance of Adequate Drainage in Raised Beds

When cultivating plants in raised beds, ensuring proper drainage is essential for their well-being. Without adequate drainage, excess water can accumulate, leading to root rot, waterlogged soil, and other problems. Olle Gardens, a trusted source for gardening advice, emphasizes the importance of drainage in raised beds.

To ensure optimal drainage in raised beds, consider the following tips:

- **Raised Bed Construction:** When building raised beds, incorporate drainage systems such as gravel-filled trenches or drainage pipes. These features facilitate the movement of excess water away from the plant roots, preventing waterlogging.
- **Soil Composition:** Use a well-draining soil mix that consists of a balanced combination of organic matter, such as compost, and coarse materials like sand or perlite. This composition helps water move through the soil more efficiently, preventing water accumulation.
- **Raised Bed Design:** Ensure that your raised bed has sufficient drainage outlets, such as drainage holes or gaps between wooden boards. This allows excess water to escape easily, preventing it from pooling within the bed.

By paying attention to proper drainage in raised beds, you can create an environment that promotes healthy root development and prevents water-related issues.

Striking a Balance

Finding the ideal balance between providing adequate water and ensuring proper drainage is key to maintaining healthy plants. It's essential to consider factors such as soil type, plant species, climate, and local weather conditions.

To achieve this balance, follow these practical tips:

- **Monitor Soil Moisture:** Regularly check the moisture levels in your soil by inserting your finger about an inch deep. If the soil feels dry at this depth, it's an indication that your plants may need watering. Conversely, if the soil feels overly saturated or wet, it may be a sign of overwatering.
- **Watering Techniques:** When watering, focus on delivering water directly to the base of the plants, aiming to saturate the root zone. This method encourages deep root growth and discourages the development of shallow roots that are more susceptible to drying out.
- **Mulching:** Applying a layer of organic mulch around the base of plants, such as straw or wood chips, helps retain soil moisture by reducing evaporation. Mulching also acts as an insulating barrier,

protecting plant roots from extreme temperature fluctuations.

- **Observe Plant Responses:** Pay attention to how your plants respond to your watering routine. Healthy plants will exhibit vibrant foliage, while signs of stress, such as wilting or yellowing leaves, may indicate inadequate watering or excessive moisture.

RAINWATER COLLECTION FOR RAISED BEDS

In today's world, where sustainability and environmental consciousness are gaining momentum, incorporating rainwater collection systems for raised beds has become a popular practice among avid gardeners. Not only does this approach offer financial savings, but it also eliminates the exposure of plants to chemicals present in tap water. In this section, we will explore the numerous benefits of rainwater collection for raised beds and provide a step-by-step guide on calculating the amount of rainwater that can be collected.

Benefits of Rainwater Collection for Raised Beds:
Collecting rainwater for raised beds offers a range of advantages that go beyond mere cost savings. Let's dive into some key benefits:

- **Environmental Friendliness:** By utilizing rainwater instead of relying solely on tap water, gardeners actively contribute to water conservation efforts. This sustainable practice helps reduce strain on local water supplies and promotes an eco-friendlier approach to gardening.

- **Chemical-Free Water:** Tap water is treated with chemicals to ensure its safety for drinking purposes. However, these chemicals can have adverse effects on the growth and health of plants. Rainwater collection eliminates this concern by providing natural and chemical-free water that is beneficial for plant growth.
- **Cost Savings:** By harnessing rainwater, gardeners can significantly reduce their water bills. Rainwater is freely available and can be used to irrigate raised beds, reducing reliance on municipal water supplies.

Calculating Rainwater Collection Potential: To determine the amount of rainwater that can be collected for your raised beds, you can follow these simple steps:

1. **Measure the Collection Surface Area.** Measure the square footage of the surface area from which rainwater will be collected. This could include rooftops, sheds, or any other suitable structures that can capture rainwater.
2. **Determine the Rainfall Harvesting Efficiency:** The efficiency of rainwater collection varies depending on factors such as guttering, downpipe capacity, and storage systems. Generally, an efficiency of 85–90% is achievable with well-designed systems.

3. **Estimate the Annual Rainfall:** Find the average annual rainfall for your location. This information is often available through local weather reports or online resources.

4. **Calculate the Rainwater Collection Potential:** Multiply the collection surface area (in square feet) by the rainfall harvesting efficiency (as a decimal) and the average annual rainfall (in inches). Convert the result into gallons for a more practical measurement.

Using Rainwater for Irrigation: Once you have collected rainwater, there are various methods for utilizing it in your raised beds:

- **Watering Can:** For small-scale gardening or precise watering needs, a watering can filled from the rainwater barrel is an excellent option. It allows you to target specific plants and control the amount of water they receive.
- **Gravity-Fed Hose:** If your rainwater storage system is elevated above your raised beds, gravity can be utilized to create water pressure. Attach a hose to the barrel's outlet and guide it to the beds for convenient irrigation.

Rainwater collection for raised beds presents an array of benefits for gardeners who are passionate about sustainability and environmental stewardship. By following the guidelines mentioned here, you can harness the advantages of rainwater, save money, and promote healthy plant growth without exposing your plants to chemicals found in tap water. Embrace this eco-friendly approach and enjoy a more sustainable gardening experience. Just make sure to check the laws in your state for restrictions on collecting and using rainwater.

ALTERNATIVE WATERING SYSTEMS FOR RAISED BEDS

When it comes to tending to raised beds, hand watering can be a viable option initially. However, it may become inadequate, particularly during the dry summer months when consistent rainfall cannot be relied upon. In such cases, alternative watering systems offer a practical and efficient solution. In this section, we will explore the benefits and drawbacks of popular options like soaker hoses, drip lines, and drip tape while providing valuable insights into their effectiveness.

Benefits and Drawbacks of Alternative Watering Systems

Soaker Hoses: Soaker hoses are porous tubes that release water directly into the soil. They offer several advantages, including:

- Efficient water distribution: Soaker hoses deliver water directly to the plant roots, minimizing waste due to evaporation and runoff.
- Deep root penetration: The slow and steady release of water promotes deep root growth, leading to healthier and more resilient plants.
- Weed suppression: By delivering water precisely to the plant roots, soaker hoses help reduce weed growth in the surrounding areas.

However, soaker hoses have some drawbacks to consider:

- Uneven water distribution: If the soil is uneven or the hoses are not properly laid out, certain areas may receive more water than others, leading to uneven plant growth.
- Clogging potential: Over time, mineral deposits or debris may clog the pores of the soaker hoses, compromising their effectiveness.

Drip Lines: Drip lines consist of small tubes with evenly spaced emitters that deliver water directly to the plants. Here are their key benefits:

- Precise watering: Drip lines provide targeted irrigation, ensuring water reaches the roots of each plant with accuracy.

- Water conservation: By minimizing water runoff and evaporation, drip lines optimize water usage and promote efficient resource management.
- Customizable configuration: Drip lines can be easily adjusted and expanded to accommodate the layout and needs of various raised bed arrangements.

However, there are a few considerations with drip lines:

- Installation complexity: Properly setting up drip lines may require some initial effort and planning to ensure optimal coverage and functionality.
- Emitter clogging: Similar to soaker hoses, drip line emitters can become clogged if not regularly inspected and maintained.

Drip Tape: Drip tape is a thin, flexible tubing with tiny, laser-cut holes that emit water directly to the plants. Here's why it's worth considering:

- Even water distribution: Drip tape provides consistent water distribution along the entire length of the tubing, ensuring uniform moisture levels for all plants.
- Cost-effective solution: Drip tape is generally affordable and can cover larger areas without compromising water efficiency.

- Easy installation: Drip tape is straightforward to install and can be adapted to fit various raised bed configurations.

However, be aware of the following considerations:

- Durability: Drip tape may not be as durable as other alternatives, and regular inspection and replacement may be necessary.
- Water pressure management: Proper water pressure regulation is crucial for the optimal functioning of the drip tape system.

Hand watering alone may prove insufficient for maintaining optimal moisture levels in raised beds, particularly during dry periods. Exploring alternative watering systems such as soaker hoses, drip lines, and drip tape can provide efficient solutions that promote healthier plant growth while conserving water. By considering the benefits and drawbacks of each system and incorporating personal experiences, you can make informed choices that align with your specific needs and gardening practices.

Interactive Element

This interactive element will be a suggestion. I personally don't have a sophisticated watering system. My yard is small, and everything is close to my house so I am happy using a watering can. I also have a hose that reaches the edge of my yard for the beds that are further away from my house.

If your beds are further away from your water source, you may need to use something more than a watering can and a hose!

Whatever works for you is going to be fine if it allows you to water your precious plants.

Rainwater collection system

In the next chapter, we will focus on planting seeds, exploring the third "P" in successful gardening.

5

PLANTING A RAISED BED GARDEN

In the words of Luther Burbank, a renowned horticulturist, "Don't wait for someone to bring you flowers. Plant your own garden and decorate your own soul." These words remind us that gardening is about taking initiative and creating something meaningful. In this chapter, we will focus on the best plants for beginners to grow in raised beds and how the concept of square-foot gardening can help you maximize your growing space.

Starting with the right plants can set the stage for a rewarding and successful experience. Raised beds offer several advantages, such as improved soil drainage, better control over soil quality, and a reduced risk of weed competition. By choosing the right plants for these beds, you can increase your chances of achieving flourishing gardens and bountiful harvests.

Throughout this chapter, we will explore a carefully curated selection of plants that are well suited for beginners' raised beds. We will consider various factors, such as their adaptability, low maintenance requirements, and the satisfaction they bring to novice gardeners. By focusing on these plants, you will gain the confidence to nurture your own garden oasis, bringing beauty and joy to your outdoor spaces.

Additionally, I will introduce the concept of square-foot gardening, a method that optimizes space utilization within raised beds. With square-foot gardening, gardeners divide their beds into individual square-foot sections, allowing for efficient use of available space and preventing overcrowding. This technique not only maximizes productivity but also simplifies garden planning and maintenance for beginners.

By the end of this chapter, you will be equipped with the knowledge and skills necessary to start different types of seeds, foster their growth, and confidently transplant them to their permanent homes within the raised beds. This newfound expertise will empower beginners to embrace the art of gardening and cultivate their own slice of nature's beauty.

So, let's dig in and get our hands dirty! We'll plant seeds, watch them grow, and soak up the joy and satisfaction that comes from tending to nature's creations.

UNDERSTANDING PLANT TYPES

In this section, we will focus on plant types—annuals, biennials, and perennials—and unravel the secrets of their life cycles. By understanding these distinct plant categories, we can enhance our gardening knowledge and make informed decisions when selecting plants for our landscapes.

- **Annual Plants:** Annual plants, as the name suggests, complete their life cycle within a single growing season. They germinate from seeds, grow into mature plants, produce flowers, set seeds, and then die. The beauty of annuals lies in their ability to burst with vibrant colors and provide an intense display of beauty throughout their relatively short lifespan. Marigolds, zinnias, petunias, and sunflowers are popular examples of annuals.
- **Biennial Plants:** Unlike annuals, biennial plants require two growing seasons to complete their life cycle. During the first year, they germinate from seeds, develop foliage, and establish a strong root system. However, they typically do not flower until the following year. Biennials require patience from gardeners, as the reward of their blooms arrives in the second year. Foxgloves, hollyhocks, sweet William, and parsley are well-known examples of biennials.

- **Perennial Plants:** Perennial plants are the backbone of many gardens, offering long-lasting beauty and stability. These plants continue to grow and reproduce for many years, with some going dormant in winter and re-emerging in spring, while others maintain their leaves throughout the year. Roses, oak trees, daisies, and hostas are just a few examples of perennials. Their enduring presence adds depth and permanence to any garden.

- **Adaptability of Annuals:** While annual plants typically complete their life cycle in a single year, it's important to note that their behavior can be influenced by climate and growing conditions. In milder regions or areas with extended growing seasons, some annuals may behave like biennials or even perennials. This adaptability offers exciting possibilities for gardeners, as they can experiment with different plant behaviors and maximize the longevity of their plantings.

Understanding the life cycles of different plant types has several implications for gardeners:

- **Designing Seasonal Displays:** Annuals, with their rapid growth and vibrant blooms, are excellent choices for creating seasonal displays. Their ability to complete their life cycle within a year allows for endless possibilities in designing flower beds, containers, and borders.

- **Planning for Succession:** Biennials require strategic planning to ensure a continuous display of blooms. By sowing seeds at different times, gardeners can stagger the growth of biennials and avoid gaps in the garden, maintaining a visually appealing landscape throughout the year.

- **Creating Long-Lasting Landscapes:** Perennials serve as the foundation for creating enduring landscapes. Their longevity provides stability and consistency, ensuring year-round interest and a sustainable garden design.

- **Adapting to Climate and Conditions:** Understanding the adaptability of annuals in different climates empowers gardeners to select appropriate plants that will thrive in their specific region. This knowledge allows for informed choices and successful gardening practices.

These different plant types offer unique characteristics and contributions to our gardens, from the fleeting beauty of annuals to the patient growth of biennials and the enduring presence of perennials. Equipped with this knowledge, we can make informed decisions when selecting plants, ensuring successful gardening endeavors, and creating stunning landscapes that evolve and thrive year after year. Let's embrace the wonders of plant life cycles, sowing the seeds of knowledge and reaping the rewards of a vibrant and flourishing garden!

IDEAL PLANTS FOR RAISED BEDS

When it comes to raised bed gardening, selecting the right plants is essential for a successful and bountiful harvest. With the advantage of improved soil drainage, better pest control, and increased accessibility, raised beds provide an ideal environment for various plants to thrive. In this section, we will explore a diverse range of plant options that are perfect for raised beds. From vibrant vegetables to luscious fruits and aromatic herbs, we will discuss the characteristics and benefits of each plant, empowering you to make informed choices for your raised bed garden.

- **Carrots**: Carrots are a popular choice for raised beds due to their ability to grow straight and deep in loose soil. They thrive in well-drained, sandy loam soil and require regular watering to prevent the roots from becoming woody.
- **Cucumbers**: Cucumbers are vining plants that benefit from the vertical space provided by raised beds. They require ample sunlight, consistent watering, and support structures for their tendrils to climb.
- **Radishes**: Radishes are quick-growing and perfect for raised beds with their small, compact roots. They

prefer well-drained soil and thrive in cool weather conditions.

- **Onions**: Onions are versatile and can be grown in raised beds. They require well-drained soil, consistent moisture, and full sun. Raised beds offer excellent drainage, which helps prevent rotting.

- **Tomatoes**: Tomatoes are a favorite among gardeners and raised beds provide an ideal environment for their growth. They require rich soil, ample sunlight, and support structures for their vines to climb.

- **Kale**: Kale is a nutritious leafy green that grows well in raised beds. It thrives in cool weather conditions and requires regular watering to maintain its crispness and flavor.

- **Lettuce**: Lettuce is a cool-season crop that grows well in raised beds. It appreciates well-drained soil and consistent moisture. Raised beds also help elevate the leaves, reducing the risk of soil-borne diseases.

- **Spinach**: Spinach is another leafy green that flourishes in raised beds. It prefers cool weather and partial shade, making it an excellent choice for early spring or fall plantings.

- **Mint**: Mint is a vigorous herb that can quickly spread if not contained. Growing mint in raised beds helps prevent it from overtaking other plants in the garden. It thrives in well-drained soil and appreciates regular watering.

- **Peas**: Peas are climbing plants that benefit from the vertical space provided by raised beds. They require support structures and prefer cool weather conditions for optimal growth.
- **Celery**: Celery is a moisture-loving plant that thrives in raised beds with consistent watering. It appreciates fertile soil and benefits from the improved drainage provided by raised beds.
- **Beets**: Beets grow well in raised beds, particularly in loose, well-drained soil. They appreciate full sun and regular watering to promote healthy root development.
- **Potatoes**: Potatoes can be successfully grown in raised beds. They require loose, well-drained soil and benefit from hilling as they grow. Raised beds make it easier to control soil moisture and provide adequate space for tuber development.
- **Arugula**: Arugula is a fast-growing green that adds a peppery flavor to salads. It thrives in raised beds, appreciating the improved drainage and the ability to harvest leaves at various stages of growth.
- **Summer Squash**: Summer squash, such as zucchini and yellow squash, are prolific growers that benefit from the nutrient-rich soil of raised beds. They require full sun, regular watering, and ample space for their sprawling vines.
- **Beans**: Beans, both bush and pole varieties, can be grown in raised beds. They require support

structures for pole beans and appreciate well-drained soil and consistent moisture.

- **Peppers**: Peppers, whether sweet or hot, thrive in raised beds with their warm soil and improved drainage. They require full sun, regular watering, and fertile soil.

- **Swiss Chard**: Swiss chard is a versatile leafy green that grows well in raised beds. It appreciates well-drained soil, partial shade in hot climates, and consistent moisture.

- **Cucamelon**: Cucamelon, also known as "mouse melon" or "Mexican sour gherkin," is a unique and flavorful vine that produces small cucumber-like fruits. It grows well in raised beds and requires support for its climbing vines.

- **Sweet Potatoes**: Sweet potatoes are root vegetables that can be grown in raised beds. They require loose, well-drained soil and consistent moisture to promote tuber development.

- **Watermelon**: Watermelons can be successfully grown in raised beds, particularly in warm climates. They require full sun, fertile soil, and ample space for their sprawling vines.

- **Eggplants**: Eggplants thrive in the warm and well-drained soil of raised beds. They require full sun, regular watering, and support structures for their heavy fruits.

- **Strawberries**: Strawberries are well-suited for raised beds, where their spreading habit can be controlled. They require full sun, well-drained soil, and regular watering.
- **Blackberries**: Blackberries can be trained on trellises or grown in raised beds with support structures. They appreciate full sun, fertile soil, and regular pruning to maintain productivity.

With a myriad of options available, selecting the ideal plants for your raised beds is a delightful journey of discovery. Whether you prefer vibrant vegetables, fragrant herbs, or luscious fruits, there is a perfect selection for every raised bed garden. By considering the specific needs and growth habits of each plant, you can create a harmonious and productive garden that brings joy and abundance. So, roll up your sleeves, dig into the soil, and embrace the satisfaction of nurturing these ideal plants in your raised bed garden.

FLOWERS TO MAKE RAISED BEDS POP

When it comes to raised bed gardening, flowers play a vital role in not only adding vibrant colors and aesthetic appeal but also serving functional purposes. While beneficial insects and pollinators are often associated with flowers, in this section we will explore the other reasons why flowers are excellent choices for raised beds. From their ability to fix soil nutrients to their extensive root systems, flowers can contribute to the overall health and productivity of your garden.

- **Marigolds**: Marigolds are a popular choice for raised beds due to their stunning colors and various benefits. They have a natural ability to repel certain pests, making them effective companions for other plants. Marigolds also act as soil fixers, enhancing soil fertility and texture with their deep root systems.
- **Borage**: Borage is an enchanting flower that not only adds beauty but also offers numerous advantages for raised beds. Its vibrant blue flowers attract pollinators, contributing to the overall health of the garden. Borage is also a dynamic accumulator, drawing up nutrients from deep in the soil and making them available to other plants.
- **Nasturtiums**: Nasturtiums are prized for their vibrant flowers and distinctive foliage. They thrive in raised beds, adding a pop of color, and acting as dynamic accumulators, pulling up nutrients and improving soil health. Nasturtiums can also deter pests such as aphids, serving as natural pest control.
- **Calendula**: Calendula, with its cheerful yellow and orange blooms, is a versatile flower for raised beds. It attracts beneficial insects and pollinators while also serving as a soil fixer. Calendula's deep root system helps break up compacted soil, improving drainage and nutrient availability.

- **Sunflowers**: Sunflowers are a classic choice for raised beds, known for their towering height and vibrant blooms. These majestic flowers not only create a visual spectacle but also act as soil conditioners. Their extensive root systems penetrate deep into the soil, improving its structure and nutrient retention.
- **Cosmos**: Cosmos is a charming flower that adds elegance and grace to raised beds. Its delicate petals and vibrant colors create a whimsical atmosphere. Cosmos is an excellent choice for attracting butterflies and other pollinators, enhancing the biodiversity of your garden.
- **Sweet Peas**: Sweet peas are beloved for their enchanting fragrance and delicate blooms. These climbers are perfect for vertical gardening in raised beds. In addition to their visual appeal, sweet peas enrich the soil with nitrogen through a process called nitrogen fixation, benefiting neighboring plants.
- **Phacelia**: Phacelia, also known as bee's friend, is a flower that excels in raised beds. Its attractive lavender-blue flowers attract bees and other pollinators, promoting a healthy ecosystem in your garden. Phacelia's deep root system helps improve soil structure and moisture retention.
- **Lupins**: Lupins are prized for their majestic flower spikes and vibrant colors. These perennial flowers

thrive in raised beds, adding vertical interest and attracting pollinators. Lupins have deep taproots that aid in soil aeration and nutrient cycling.

- **Clover**: Clover is a versatile flower that offers numerous benefits for raised beds. Its dense foliage acts as a living mulch, suppressing weeds and conserving soil moisture. Clover is a nitrogen-fixing plant, enriching the soil with this essential nutrient.

Flowers are not only a feast for the eyes but also valuable contributors to the functionality and productivity of raised beds. Marigolds, borage, nasturtiums, calendula, sunflowers, cosmos, sweet peas, phacelia, lupins, and clover are just a few examples of the wide variety of flowers that can make your raised beds pop. Their ability to fix soil nutrients, improve soil structure, attract pollinators, and deter pests makes them indispensable additions to any raised bed garden. So, unleash your creativity, select your favorite flowers, and watch your raised beds transform into vibrant and thriving havens of beauty and functionality.

WHAT IS SQUARE-FOOT GARDENING?

Square-foot gardening is a popular gardening method that offers an efficient and organized approach to growing plants. It is particularly beneficial for beginners as it provides a clear understanding of how much can be planted in a given area without overcrowding or wasting valuable space. By following a few simple principles and techniques, square-foot gardening allows gardeners to make the most of their available space, resulting in a bountiful and manageable harvest. In this section, we will discuss the key aspects of square-foot gardening, including crop layout planning, determining the right number of crops per square foot, considering plant height, and incorporating grids for better organization and rotation.

Plan Your Crop Layout

One of the foundations of square-foot gardening is careful planning of the crop layout. By dividing the garden into square-foot sections, you can strategically arrange your crops for optimal growth and utilization of space. Consider the specific requirements of each plant, such as sunlight exposure, water needs, and compatibility with neighboring plants. This planning stage ensures the efficient use of resources and minimizes the risk of overcrowding.

Plan the Right Number of Crops per Square Foot

A key aspect of square-foot gardening is determining the appropriate number of plants to grow within each square foot. This is typically based on a planting guide that follows a specific spacing pattern. For example, the 16/9/8/4/2/1 grid system suggests planting 16 plants per square foot for small plants like radishes, 9 plants for plants with a slightly larger footprint like carrots, 8 plants for onions, 4 plants for larger plants like lettuce or spinach, 2 plants for larger herbs or dwarf fruit plants, and finally, 1 plant for larger vegetables such as tomatoes or peppers. Following these guidelines ensures that each plant has sufficient space to thrive.

Keep height in mind: When planning your square-foot garden, it is crucial to consider the height of the plants you intend to grow. Taller plants should be placed in areas where they won't shade smaller plants or hinder their growth. By arranging plants based on their height requirements, you can ensure that all plants receive adequate sunlight and air circulation, promoting healthy development and preventing shading-related issues.

Add the Grids

Grids play a significant role in square-foot gardening as they provide a clear visual guide for planting and organization. The grids can be created using materials such as wooden slats or string, dividing the garden into equal square-foot sections. These grids not only help maintain the appropriate spacing between plants but also aid in crop rotation, pest management, and general garden maintenance.

Rotate Crops in Squares

Crop rotation is an essential practice in any garden, including square-foot gardens. By rotating crops within the square-foot sections, you can minimize the risk of soil-borne diseases, optimize nutrient uptake, and promote overall plant health. For example, in one square-foot section, you can grow tomatoes one year, followed by cucumbers the next year, and then beans in subsequent years. This rotation helps break the pest and disease cycles and maintain soil fertility.

HOW TO START SEEDS

It's an incredibly rewarding experience to witness the transformation of tiny seeds into flourishing plants. However, with the vast array of plants available and the variations in climate zones, it's essential to understand how and when to start seeds. Fear not, for I will guide you through the process, ensuring your gardening endeavors are met with success.

First and foremost, let's unravel the valuable information found on a seed packet. When you hold a seed packet in your hands, you possess a treasure trove of knowledge. The packet serves as a gateway to understanding the specific requirements of the seeds within. Let's explore the key details typically provided on a seed packet:

- **Plant Variety and Scientific Name:** The seed packet will clearly indicate the plant variety and its scientific name. This information helps you identify the exact type of plant you are dealing with and ensures accuracy in your gardening journey.

- **Sowing and Germination Instructions:** One of the most critical aspects of seed starting is knowing when and how to sow them. The packet will outline the optimal time to plant the seeds based on your local climate and frost dates. It may provide recommendations for indoor or outdoor sowing, depth of planting, and spacing between seeds.

- **Light and Temperature Requirements:** Different plants have distinct preferences when it comes to light and temperature conditions. The seed packet will provide guidelines on the amount of sunlight needed and the ideal temperature range for successful germination and growth. Pay close attention to these recommendations to provide the optimal environment for your seeds.

- **Soil and Fertilizer Suggestions:** To thrive, seeds require the right soil composition and nutrients. The packet may offer advice on the soil type, pH level, and amendments needed for optimal growth. Additionally, it may suggest specific fertilizers or organic matter to enhance the soil fertility and support healthy plant development.

- **Watering Instructions:** Water is a lifeline for seeds, and the seed packet will provide guidance on watering practices. It may suggest regular watering intervals, emphasizing the importance of maintaining consistent moisture levels without overwatering. This information is crucial for preventing seed rot or drought stress.

- **Days to Germination and Maturity:** The seed packet often includes an estimate of the time it takes for the seeds to germinate and the duration until the plant reaches maturity. This information allows you to plan your gardening activities, monitor progress, and anticipate when you can expect to enjoy the fruits of your labor.

- **Additional Tips and Precautions:** Seed packets often include additional tidbits of wisdom to increase your chances of success. These may include recommendations for thinning seedlings, providing support structures, protecting against pests, or managing common diseases. Take note of these valuable tips to overcome potential challenges along the way.

Now that you understand the wealth of information contained within a seed packet, it's time to put this knowledge into action. Let's explore a step-by-step guide on how to start seeds successfully:

1. **Gather Your Materials:** Before diving into seed starting, gather the necessary materials: seed packets, seed trays or pots, high-quality seed-starting mix, labels, a spray bottle for watering, and a warm and well-lit area for germination.

2. **Read and Understand the Seed Packets:** Carefully read the instructions on each seed packet, paying close attention to sowing depth, recommended indoor or outdoor planting, and any specific requirements unique to the plant variety.

3. **Prepare Your Seed Trays or Pots:** Fill your seed trays or pots with a sterile seed-starting mix, leaving a small gap at the top for watering. Moisten the mix with a fine mist using a spray bottle, ensuring it is evenly moist but not saturated.

4. **Sow the Seeds:** Following the seed packet instructions, sow the seeds at the recommended depth. Label each tray or pot to keep track of the planted varieties.

5. **Provide Optimal Growing Conditions:** Place your seed trays or pots in a warm location with ample light. Ensure the seeds receive the appropriate amount of sunlight or use artificial grow lights if necessary. Maintain the recommended temperature and moisture levels as specified on the seed packets.

6. **Care for Seedlings:** As the seeds germinate, monitor their progress closely. Thin out overcrowded seedlings if needed, providing ample space for healthy growth. Water the seedlings gently and regularly, ensuring the soil remains consistently moist but not waterlogged.

7. **Harden Off and Transplant:** When the seedlings have developed sufficient strength and size,

gradually expose them to outdoor conditions through a process called hardening off. This helps them acclimate to the change in environment before transplanting them into your garden.

8. **Plant in the Garden:** Following the appropriate outdoor planting dates and spacing recommendations, transplant the seedlings into your garden beds or containers. Remember to provide adequate support, mulch as needed, and continue to care for them as they grow.

By following these steps and utilizing the information provided on seed packets, you'll set yourself up for a successful seed-starting adventure. Embrace the excitement of nurturing seeds into healthy plants and watch as your garden flourishes with life.

TRANSPLANTING SEEDLINGS

Transplanting seedlings is a pivotal step in cultivating your garden. When your seedlings have reached a height of 2 to 3 inches and possess at least two true leaves, they are ready for the next phase of their growth. In this guide, we will explore the necessary steps for successful transplanting, ensuring your precious seedlings thrive in their new outdoor home.

Before we talk about the transplanting process, let's discuss the importance of hardening off. When seedlings are grown indoors, they are sheltered from the harsh elements of the outdoor environment. Hardening off is the process of gradually acclimating these tender plants to outdoor conditions, preventing transplant shock, and allowing for a smoother transition.

Here's how to effectively harden off your seedlings:

1. **Start Gradually:** Begin by exposing your seedlings to the outdoors for short periods, starting with just a few hours in a shaded area. Gradually increase the time spent outside over the course of one to two weeks.

2. **Select the Right Conditions:** Ensure that the outdoor temperatures and weather conditions are suitable for your seedlings. Avoid extreme heat, strong winds, or cold snaps during the hardening-off process. Shelter the seedlings from direct sunlight initially, gradually increasing their exposure as they adapt.

3. **Protect Seedlings Overnight:** During the hardening-off period, it's important to protect your seedlings from sudden drops in temperature. Bring them indoors or provide protective coverings, such as row covers or cold frames, overnight until they are fully acclimated to outdoor temperatures.

Now that your seedlings have undergone the necessary hardening-off process, they are ready to be transplanted into their permanent garden location. Let's explore the step-by-step instructions for successful transplanting:

1. **Choose the Right Time:** Transplant your seedlings into the garden when the soil has warmed up and all risk of frost has passed. Consult your local frost dates and gardening resources to determine the optimal time for transplanting in your region.

2. **Prepare the Soil:** Ensure that the planting area is well prepared. Remove any weeds or debris and amend the soil with organic matter if necessary. This will provide a fertile and welcoming environment for your seedlings.

3. **Dig the Planting Hole:** Dig a hole in the garden bed that is slightly larger and deeper than the root ball of your seedling. Gently loosen the soil around the hole to promote root growth.

4. **Remove Seedlings From Containers:** Carefully remove the seedlings from their containers, taking care not to damage the delicate roots. Gently tease the roots apart if they are root-bound, allowing them to spread out in the planting hole.

5. **Plant Seedlings:** Place the seedling into the prepared hole, ensuring that the soil level of the garden matches the level of the soil in the container. Firmly but gently press the soil around the seedling, eliminating air pockets and providing stability.

6. **Water and Mulch:** Immediately after planting, water the seedlings thoroughly, ensuring that the soil around them is evenly moist. Apply a layer of organic mulch around the base of the seedlings to retain moisture and suppress weeds.

7. **Provide Support:** If your seedlings are tall or delicate, consider providing support to prevent them from bending or breaking in strong winds. Use stakes, cages, or trellises, depending on the plant's growth habit.

8. **Monitor and Maintain:** Keep a close eye on your transplanted seedlings during the initial days and weeks. Ensure they receive adequate water, sunlight, and protection from pests. Regularly monitor their growth and provide any necessary care, such as fertilization or pruning.

Remember, each plant has its own unique requirements, so it's essential to research specific varieties and their preferred growing conditions.

Interactive Element

Checklist: Starting Seeds to Transplanting

Prepare the Soil:

- Clear the planting area of any weeds or debris.
- Amend the soil with organic matter if needed.

Gather Supplies:

- High-quality seeds of desired plant varieties
- Seed-starting trays or pots
- Fresh potting soil
- Labels or markers
- Watering can or spray bottle

Start Seeds:

- Sow seeds according to the packet instructions.
- Maintain appropriate moisture and temperature levels.
- Provide adequate light or use artificial grow lights.

Harden Off:

- Gradually introduce seedlings to outdoor conditions.
- Increase exposure to sunlight and outdoor temperatures over one to two weeks.
- Protect seedlings from extreme weather or temperature fluctuations.

Choose the Right Time:

- Determine the optimal planting time based on your climate and local frost dates.
- Consult gardening resources for guidance.

Prepare the planting area:

- Plan your raised beds and desired planting locations.
- Ensure the soil is well prepared and free from weeds and debris.

Dig planting holes:

- Dig holes slightly larger and deeper than the root balls of the seedlings.
- Loosen the soil around the holes for better root growth.

Transplant Seedlings:

- Gently remove seedlings from their containers, taking care not to damage the roots.
- Place the seedlings into the prepared holes at the same soil level as in their containers.
- Firmly but gently press the soil around the seedlings, eliminating air pockets.

Water and Mulch:

- Immediately water the transplanted seedlings thoroughly.
- Apply a layer of organic mulch around the base of the plants to retain moisture and suppress weeds.

Monitor and maintain:

- Keep a close eye on the transplanted seedlings.
- Provide regular water, sunlight, and protection from pests.
- Monitor growth and provide necessary care, such as fertilization or pruning.

Remember to use your garden planner to map out your raised beds and keep track of your planting locations. This will help you stay organized and make the most of your gardening space. Get creative with companion planting and take note of plant spacing requirements.

In the following chapter, we will discuss the art of caring for plants in raised beds to promote vibrant and healthy growth. Stay tuned for valuable tips and techniques to enhance your gardening experience.

PASSING IT ON

— HELEN MIRREN

There's a 7th P we haven't talked about – and honestly, it doesn't have quite the same ring to it as planning, preparing, planting, parenting, pairing, or protection, so it's like a bonus extra.

You might recall that my interest in gardening grew from my parents'. They passed their wisdom and passion onto me, and this was the foundation for everything I learned afterwards… and now it's my mission to pass that wisdom on to others.

So have you figured out what that 7th P is? That's right: It's 'passing it on'. You see why it doesn't really fit with the others. Nonetheless, it's important. Keeping this knowledge alive and sharing it is how we make sure gardening thrives as a pastime – it's how we spread the joy and fulfillment it can bring, as well as doing our bit for the planet.

You'll find that this comes naturally the more you spend time gardening. You'll get into a conversation with someone while you're buying seeds, or you'll get talking to a neighbor over the fence. You'll learn a ton of useful tips this way – and you'll pass on a load too.

But there's something you can do right now to help me pass on the knowledge I first got from my parents – and the best part is, it'll only take a few minutes.

By leaving a review of this book on Amazon, you'll show other new gardeners where they can find everything they need to get a handle on the 6 Ps and start a thriving raised bed garden.

Simply by letting other readers know how this book has helped you and what they'll find inside, you'll show them exactly where they can find the same information that's helping you.

Scan the QR code to leave your review!

Thank you for your support. Now let's return to the original 6 Ps!

6

PARENTING SEEDLINGS INTO THRIVING PLANTS

Many passionate gardeners have been known to form unique bonds with their green companions. In fact, there's a touch of sanity in this seemingly "crazy" act of talking to plants. Fortunately, science has come to our rescue, confirming that we are not entirely off our rockers when engaging in such conversations. But what lies beyond these amusing exchanges?

In this chapter, we will uncover the art of pruning, a skill that plays a vital role in promoting healthy plant growth. Through proper pruning techniques, you can shape your plants, encourage new growth, and maintain their overall well-being. From understanding the different types of cuts to knowing when and how to prune various plant species, we will provide you with the knowledge and confidence to master the art of pruning.

Beyond pruning, we will explore the joy of harvesting the fruits of your labor. There's nothing quite as satisfying as plucking a ripe tomato from the vine or harvesting a basket of freshly grown herbs for a delectable recipe. We will guide you to the optimal time to harvest different vegetables, fruits, and herbs, ensuring peak flavor and nutritional value.

But the journey doesn't end there. As responsible gardeners, we understand the importance of sustainability and self-sufficiency. That's why we will talk all about the topic of seed saving. You'll learn how to collect and store seeds from your harvest, allowing you to continue the cycle of growth and abundance in the following seasons. Seed saving is not only a practical and economical approach but also a way to preserve heirloom varieties and maintain biodiversity.

Lastly, we will explore the difference between perennial and annual care, shedding light on the behavior of plants during the dormant winter months. Understanding the needs of perennial plants that persist year after year and those that complete their life cycle in a single growing season will empower you to provide the appropriate care and make informed decisions in your garden.

TAKE SOME TIME TO OBSERVE AND ENJOY

As I stroll through my garden, a place where nature and tranquility intertwine, I find solace in observing the beauty that surrounds me. It's not always about the tireless work of tending to my raised beds; it's the simple act of pausing, marveling, and appreciating the wonders that nature has bestowed upon us. In this section, inspired by the insightful musings from the resource "The Importance of Observation in the Garden," I invite you to join me on a journey of reflection, understanding, and finding joy in the art of observation.

A Story of Marveling at Growth

The importance of taking the time to observe is best illustrated by a personal experience that I'd like to share with you. As the seasons changed, my raised beds transformed from barren landscapes to vibrant patches of life. One early morning, with a steaming cup of tea in hand, I sat on the patio, gazing at the garden. Instead of immediately reaching for my gardening tools, I allowed myself to take in the scene before me. The sunlight cast a golden glow, illuminating the dew-kissed petals while delicate tendrils reached skyward. At that moment, I realized that observing the garden was just as rewarding as tending to it.

The Power of Observation

In our fast-paced lives, we often overlook the significance of observation. However, taking the time to observe can deepen our connection with nature and foster a greater understanding of the intricate web of life. When we slow down and embrace the art of observation, we become attuned to the subtle changes and rhythms that occur in our surroundings. It is through observation that we gain insights into the needs of our plants, detect potential issues, and witness the miraculous transformation from seed to harvest.

Observation as a Learning Tool

Observation is not merely a passive act; it is a valuable tool for learning and growth. By closely observing our garden, we become students of nature, constantly expanding our knowledge, and honing our skills. As we notice the intricate details of plant growth, we learn to identify the delicate balance between sunlight, water, and nutrients. We develop a keen eye for detecting pests or diseases, allowing us to take proactive measures. Moreover, observation teaches us patience and humility, reminding us that nature follows its own timeline and that not all processes can be rushed.

Finding Joy in the Details

Every garden holds hidden treasures, waiting to be discovered through observation. The true enchantment of nature can be found in the little things. As you take a closer look at the intricate patterns on a flower petal or the delicate symmetry of a butterfly's wings, you unlock a world of wonder and awe. Each leaf, each bud, and each blade of grass has a story to tell, and by taking the time to observe, we become avid storytellers, connecting deeply with the natural world around us.

Creating Moments of Reflection

Observation in the garden provides us with precious moments of reflection and introspection. It becomes a meditative practice, offering respite from the chaos of daily life. As we engage our senses and immerse ourselves in the sights, sounds, and scents of the garden, we find ourselves in a state of mindfulness. The worries and stresses melt away, replaced by a sense of calm and serenity. These moments of reflection become an essential part of self-care, nurturing our well-being, and rejuvenating our spirits.

WHY AND HOW TO PRUNE PLANTS

Pruning is an essential practice in the art of gardening, offering numerous benefits to plants, trees, and shrubs. By removing specific branches and stems, pruning promotes overall plant health, enhances air circulation, stimulates fresh growth, and maintains desired shapes. In this section, we will explore the reasons behind pruning and dig into a step-by-step guide on how to effectively prune various garden plants, excluding perennials.

The Benefits of Pruning:

- **Plant Health:** Pruning plays a pivotal role in maintaining the health and vitality of plants. By selectively removing dead, damaged, or diseased branches, we prevent the spread of infections and infestations throughout the plant, safeguarding its overall well-being.

- **Air Circulation:** Proper air circulation is crucial for plant health, as it reduces the risk of fungal diseases and promotes efficient transpiration. Pruning opens up the canopy, allowing air to freely circulate among the branches and foliage, creating a healthier environment for growth.

- **Encouraging New Growth:** Pruning stimulates the development of fresh growth. By strategically removing certain branches or stems, we redirect the plant's energy toward the remaining portions, encouraging the emergence of new buds and shoots.

- **Maintaining Desired Shapes:** Pruning enables us to shape and control the growth of plants, trees, and shrubs, ensuring they adhere to the desired form and size. Through careful and selective pruning, we can create visually appealing structures and maintain a harmonious garden layout.

Knowing the ideal time to prune different plants is essential to maximizing their growth potential. Here is a general guide:

- **Spring-flowered plants:** Prune immediately after they finish flowering. This allows sufficient time for new growth to develop and flower buds to form for the following year.
- **Summer-flowered plants:** Prune in late winter or early spring before new growth emerges. This ensures that the plant will produce vigorous shoots, resulting in abundant blooms during the summer.
- **Deciduous trees:** Prune in late winter or early spring when the tree is dormant. This minimizes the risk of disease transmission and allows the tree to allocate energy toward healing and new growth.
- **Evergreen trees and shrubs:** Pruning can be done throughout the year, but it is generally recommended to prune in late winter or early spring to coincide with the onset of new growth.

Step-by-Step Guide to Pruning:

1. Gather the necessary tools, including sharp pruning shears, loppers, and a pruning saw for larger branches. Ensure that the tools are clean and well maintained.

2. Identify the branches that require pruning. Look for dead, damaged, or crossing branches, as well as any growth that compromises the desired shape or interferes with other plants.

3. Make clean cuts at a slight angle just above a bud or lateral branch. This promotes proper healing and prevents water accumulation on the cut surface.

4. For larger branches, use a three-cut technique to avoid tearing the bark. Make an undercut first, followed by a top cut slightly further along the branch, and finally, remove the stub by making a final cut just outside the branch collar.

5. Regularly step back and assess the plant's overall shape as you prune, ensuring symmetry and balance in its appearance.

6. Dispose of pruned branches and debris responsibly, either through composting or appropriate green waste disposal methods.

Pruning is a fundamental practice for maintaining healthy and aesthetically pleasing garden plants. By understanding the benefits of pruning, knowing when to prune, and following a systematic approach, you can nurture your plants, trees, and shrubs to flourish. Remember, each pruning cut is an opportunity for growth and rejuvenation, shaping your garden into a thriving oasis of natural beauty. So, grab your gardening gloves and your pruning tools; it's time to shape up your plants and make them thrive!

THE IMPORTANCE OF DEADHEADING FLOWERS

As gardening enthusiasts, we all strive to create vibrant and captivating flower gardens that bring joy and beauty to our outdoor spaces. One essential practice that often goes unnoticed but plays a significant role in maintaining the vitality and allure of our flower beds is deadheading. In this section, we will explore the importance of deadheading flowers, the plants that benefit from this practice, and the various methods of deadheading to ensure optimal growth and prolonged blooming.

Understanding Deadheading

Deadheading is a simple yet impactful technique that involves the removal of fading or spent flowers from plants. By snipping or pinching off these spent blooms, we redirect the plant's energy toward producing new flowers and promoting overall growth. Our garden's aesthetic appeal is improved by this method, which also guarantees that it will remain healthy during the blooming season.

Benefits of Deadheading

Promotes Extended Bloom Periods

Deadheading encourages plants to produce more blooms by preventing the formation of seeds. By removing spent flowers, we prevent the plant from channeling its energy into seed production and instead redirect it toward the development of new buds. This results in an extended period of vibrant blooms, keeping our gardens filled with color and charm.

Enhances Aesthetic Appeal

By removing fading flowers, we eliminate unsightly elements from our garden beds, maintaining a neat and visually pleasing appearance. Deadheading not only contributes to the overall attractiveness of our flower gardens but also allows the remaining flowers to shine and become the focal points of our landscape.

Plants That Benefit From Deadheading

Several plant varieties greatly benefit from regular deadheading. These include, but are not limited to, the following:

- **Roses**: Deadheading roses promote continuous flowering throughout the growing season. By removing spent blooms, we encourage the growth of new buds, ensuring a stunning display of roses in our garden.
- **Marigolds**: Pinching off faded marigold flowers prevents the formation of seeds and encourages the development of new flowers, extending their blooming period.

- **Petunias**: These popular annuals respond well to deadheading. By removing wilted or spent flowers, we stimulate the production of fresh blooms, resulting in a fuller and more vibrant display.

Methods of Deadheading

There are two primary methods for deadheading flowers: pinching and cutting.

- **Pinching**: This technique involves using your fingertips or pruners to gently pinch off the faded flower heads. It is particularly effective for plants with delicate stems and smaller flowers, such as marigolds and petunias.
- **Cutting**: For plants with tougher stems or larger flower heads, a pair of sharp pruning shears or scissors can be used to make clean cuts just above a healthy leaf node or bud. This method is commonly employed for roses, where precision and care are necessary to encourage new growth.

Deadheading flowers is an essential practice that every gardener should embrace to maximize the beauty and longevity of their flower gardens. By removing faded blooms, we redirect the plant's energy toward producing new flowers, resulting in extended bloom periods and a visually captivating garden.

TIPS FOR HARVESTING FOOD

As gardeners, there is nothing more satisfying than reaping the fruits of our labor and enjoying a bountiful harvest from our carefully tended plants. Harvesting food from our gardens not only provides us with fresh, flavorful produce but also allows us to fully experience the rewards of our hard work and dedication. In this section, we will explore a collection of valuable tips and guidelines to help you optimize your food harvesting process, ensuring that you make the most of your garden's abundance.

1. **Timing Is Key:** One of the most crucial aspects of harvesting food is determining the right time to pick each crop. Timing varies for different plants, and harvesting at the optimal stage ensures the best flavor, texture, and nutritional content. Consult seed packets, gardening guides, or online resources specific to each crop for guidance on when to harvest.

2. **Gentle Handling:** Handle harvested produce with care to prevent damage and preserve its quality. Use pruners, shears, or a sharp knife to cut fruits, vegetables, or herbs from the plant rather than pulling or twisting them, which can cause unnecessary stress. Place harvested items in a basket or container lined with a soft material to cushion them during transportation.

3. **Harvesting Leafy Greens:** When harvesting leafy greens such as lettuce, spinach, or kale, selectively pluck the mature outer leaves while allowing the inner leaves to continue growing. This practice, known as "cut and come again," enables a continuous supply of fresh greens throughout the growing season.

4. **Storing Root Crops:** Root crops like carrots, beets, and potatoes can be stored for an extended period if harvested and handled correctly. Trim the foliage, gently remove extra soil, and keep them in a cool, dark, and well-ventilated area to maintain their freshness. Consider using breathable containers or crates to prevent moisture buildup.

5. **Vine Crops and Fruiting Vegetables:** Harvest vine crops, such as cucumbers, squash, and melons, when they have reached their mature size but are still firm. Using a sharp knife or pruners, these produce items should be removed from the vine while still having a small stem attached. Wait until the appropriate color is obtained before carefully twisting or cutting fruits like tomatoes and peppers from the vine.

6. **Harvesting Herbs:** To harvest herbs like basil, mint, or cilantro, selectively pluck leaves from the plant, starting with the outer ones. This encourages continued growth and ensures a fresh supply of aromatic herbs throughout the season. Alternatively,

you can cut the entire stem just above a leaf node, promoting bushier growth.

7. **Regular Harvesting:** Frequent harvesting promotes continuous production and prevents plants from becoming overripe or going to seed prematurely. Regularly check your garden for ripe produce, aiming to harvest at the peak of ripeness to enjoy the best flavors and textures.

8. **Enjoy Freshness:** Whenever possible, consume freshly harvested produce immediately to savor the flavors at their peak. Whether it's a refreshing salad, a vibrant stir-fry, or a flavorful salsa, incorporating garden-fresh ingredients into your meals will elevate your culinary experiences.

9. **Sharing and Preserving the Harvest:** If your garden produces an abundance of food, consider sharing your harvest with friends, family, or local food banks. Additionally, explore various preservation methods such as canning, freezing, or drying to extend the enjoyment of your homegrown produce beyond the growing season.

By following these tips for harvesting food, you can make the most of your garden's abundance and ensure the freshest and most flavorful produce on your plate. Remember to harvest at the appropriate stage for each crop, handle your harvest with care, and incorporate it into delicious meals to fully appreciate the rewards of your gardening efforts.

SAVING YOUR SEEDS

One of the most rewarding aspects of gardening is the opportunity to save and preserve seeds from our favorite plants. By saving seeds, we not only ensure the continuity of beloved varieties but also empower ourselves to become self-reliant and resilient gardeners. In this section, we will explore the art of seed saving and provide you with essential tips and guidelines to help you successfully save and store different types of seeds. Remember, proper drying and storage are key to maintaining seed viability and preventing issues like bacteria or mold. Let's learn about seed saving and discover how to preserve the future of your garden.

Saving Vegetable Seeds

When it comes to saving vegetable seeds, it's essential to start with open-pollinated or heirloom varieties. Seeds from hybrid plants do not grow true to their parent plant. Select healthy, fully mature fruits for seed saving. For tomatoes and cucumbers, scoop out the seeds and allow them to ferment in a container for a few days. Rinse the seeds thoroughly, dry them on a paper towel, and store them in labeled envelopes or jars in a cool, dry place.

Saving Flower Seeds

To save flower seeds, choose healthy, vibrant blooms that have completed their lifecycle. Make sure the seeds inside the flowers are fully developed by allowing them to wilt and dry on the plant. Gently collect the dried flower heads, remove the seeds, and separate them from any debris or chaff. Place the seeds on a paper plate or screen to dry thoroughly for a week or two before transferring them to envelopes or small containers for storage.

Saving Herb Seeds

Herb seeds can be easily saved by allowing the plants to flower and go to seed. Carefully gather the seed heads and put them in a paper bag once they have dried and gone brown. Separate the seeds from the chaff after shaking the bag to release the seeds from the seed heads. Store the cleaned seeds in labeled envelopes or containers, ensuring they are completely dry.

Drying and Storing Seeds

Proper drying and storage are crucial for seed longevity. After collecting the seeds, ensure they are thoroughly dried before storing. On a piece of paper, a screen, or a mesh surface, spread the seeds out in a single layer. Place them away from direct sunshine in a well-ventilated place and give them several weeks to thoroughly dry. Once dry, transfer the seeds to labeled envelopes or airtight containers. Store them in a cool, dark, and dry location, such as a refrigerator or a cool basement, to maintain their viability.

Labeling and Documentation

Accurate labeling is essential for seed saving. Clearly mark each envelope or container with the plant variety, date of collection, and any additional relevant information. Consider creating a seed-saving journal or spreadsheet to document your seed-saving endeavors, including details such as plant characteristics, growing conditions, and any observations or notes that may be helpful for future reference.

Sharing and Exchanging Seeds

Seed saving also offers a wonderful opportunity for community building and sharing with other gardeners. Consider participating in seed exchanges or sharing your saved seeds with friends and fellow enthusiasts. Sharing seeds not only fosters diversity but also strengthens the collective knowledge and resilience of gardeners worldwide.

Testing Seed Viability

Over time, seed viability may decrease. To ensure successful germination, periodically test the viability of stored seeds. A tiny sample of seeds should be placed on a damp paper towel, sealed in a plastic bag, and stored in a warm place for a week. Check the seeds for germination rates. If the majority of seeds sprout, they are still viable for planting. If germination rates are low, it may be time to replace those seeds with fresh ones.

Saving your own seeds is a rewarding and empowering practice that allows you to nurture a continuous cycle of growth in your garden. By following proper seed-saving techniques and storing them in optimal conditions, you can preserve the genetic diversity of your plants and maintain a self-sustaining garden for years to come. Remember, each saved seed carries with it the potential for new life and bountiful harvests.

WHAT TO DO AS WINTER APPROACHES

As the air turns crisp and the days grow shorter, it's time to prepare our gardens for the impending arrival of winter. Taking proactive steps to protect and care for our plants during this transitional period ensures their health and vitality, setting the stage for a successful growing season ahead. In this section, we will outline five key steps to prepare your garden beds for winter, providing you with the knowledge and guidance you need to safeguard your plants and optimize their winter survival. Additionally, we will touch upon the benefits and strategies for utilizing raised beds during the colder months. Below you will discover how to prepare your garden for the approaching winter:

1. **Clearing and Cleanup:** Begin by removing any spent annuals or diseased plants from your garden beds. Eliminate weeds, debris, and fallen leaves that could be a breeding ground for pests and diseases. This thorough cleaning process helps prevent the overwintering of pests and creates a clean canvas for the upcoming season.

2. **Soil Amendment and Mulching:** Enhance the soil's fertility and structure by amending it with organic matter. Spread a layer of compost, well-rotted manure, or leaf mold over the surface of the beds and gently work it into the top few inches of soil. This enriches the soil, promotes beneficial microbial activity, and replenishes essential nutrients. Additionally, apply a layer of organic mulch, such as straw or wood chips, to help insulate the soil and protect it from temperature fluctuations.

3. **Protecting Perennials:** Insulate and shield your perennial plants from harsh winter conditions. Herbaceous perennials' stems should be pruned back to a few inches above the ground. To add an additional layer of defense, spread mulch around

their bases. For more delicate perennials, consider covering them with burlap or frost blankets to safeguard them from freezing temperatures and frost damage.

4. **Pruning and Trimming:** Some trees, shrubs, and vines can be pruned in the late fall. To enhance the overall structure and promote healthy development, cut back any dead, broken, or crossed branches. However, be cautious not to prune spring-blooming plants that set buds on old wood. Consult specific pruning guidelines for different plant varieties to ensure proper timing and technique.

5. **Irrigation and Drainage:** Properly manage irrigation and drainage systems to prevent waterlogging and potential damage during the winter. Before freezing temperatures set in, drain and store garden hoses, ensuring no water remains inside. Additionally, consider installing protective covers or insulating materials around outdoor faucets to prevent freezing and potential pipe damage. Evaluate the garden's drainage to address any areas prone to water pooling or excessive runoff, making necessary adjustments to promote proper water flow.

As you follow these steps to prepare your garden beds for winter, it's important to note that raised beds offer unique advantages in terms of soil warmth, drainage, and protection against frost.

Interactive Element

We have designed a garden calendar planner to make it easier for you to stay organized and keep track of your gardening chores. This interactive tool will enable you to monitor what you planted, record important dates, and manage your garden effectively.

With the garden calendar planner, you will have a comprehensive tool to manage your garden and ensure that you stay on top of your planting schedule. Utilize this interactive tool to improve your gardening abilities and have success in your garden.

Start Date	Annual	Biennial	Perennial	Notes

Just because some plants go dormant in winter doesn't mean that raised beds have to remain lifeless. While the colder months bring challenges to gardening, there are plenty of ways to keep your raised beds attractive, colorful, and productive. In the upcoming chapter, we are going to look at ways to keep raised beds looking attractive, colorful, and productive in the colder months.

7

HOW TO KEEP YOUR RAISED BEDS BLOOMING IN WINTER

When winter arrives, it's easy to assume that your raised beds will become dormant and devoid of color. However, with the right strategies and plant selections, you can keep your raised beds blooming and vibrant even during the colder months. Whether you're interested in extending the growing season or simply want to add some visual interest to your garden, there are options available to suit your preferences.

If you're not particularly keen on extending the growing season and prefer to focus on crops that can withstand the cold weather, there are still plenty of choices available. Some cold-hardy vegetables, such as kale, Swiss chard, and Brussels sprouts, can thrive in winter conditions. These resilient plants can withstand frost and continue to provide fresh and nutritious harvests throughout the season.

Additionally, consider planting winter herbs like rosemary, thyme, and sage, which can add both beauty and flavor to your raised beds.

Covering your raised beds is crucial to protecting your plants from the severe winter temperatures. By providing a layer of insulation, you can shield your plants from freezing temperatures, wind, and frost. There are various methods to cover your raised beds, including using row covers, cloches, or even constructing mini greenhouses. These covers create a microclimate that traps warmth and shields your plants from the elements, allowing them to thrive and continue blooming.

Remember to choose appropriate cover materials that allow for airflow and light penetration. This helps prevent the buildup of excess moisture, which can lead to fungal diseases. Keep an eye out for pests and illnesses in your plants on a regular basis and take the necessary precautions to minimize any potential problems.

By embracing the beauty of winter gardening and utilizing the right techniques, you can create a captivating display in your raised beds, even during the quieter months. So, don't let the winter season dampen your gardening enthusiasm. As Rumi once said, "Don't think the garden loses its ecstasy in winter. It's quiet, but the roots are down there, riotous." Embrace the riotous roots and discover the enchantment that winter can bring to your raised beds.

Stay tuned for the upcoming chapter, where we will dig deeper into the wonders of winter gardening and explore additional strategies to enhance your raised beds during this season of tranquility and growth.

PLANTS THAT DO BETTER IN WINTER

When it comes to gardening, many people associate it with spring and summer, envisioning vibrant blooms and bountiful harvests. However, the winter season also offers ample opportunities to cultivate a diverse range of plants that not only survive but thrive in colder temperatures. In this section, we will explore the benefits of planting certain crops and flowers during the fall season, allowing them to flourish throughout the winter months.

One key aspect of winter gardening is understanding the ideal planting time for certain crops. Onions and garlic, for example, are best planted in the fall. While they may appear dormant during the winter, their roots have sufficient time to establish themselves in the soil. When spring arrives, these plants quickly sprout shoots and are ready for harvesting earlier than if they were planted in the spring. By planning ahead and sowing these crops in the fall, gardeners can enjoy an early harvest and savor the flavors of freshly grown onions and garlic.

In addition to onions and garlic, several cool-season crops thrive in winter conditions. Plants such as kale, lettuce, spinach, and Swiss chard are well-suited to colder temperatures and can even benefit from the protection of raised beds with covers. These covers help create a microclimate that shields the plants from harsh winter elements while providing them with the ideal growing environment. By embracing the winter season, gardeners can enjoy a continuous supply of nutrient-rich greens and add a touch of freshness to their winter meals.

Root vegetables also fare exceptionally well when planted in the fall. Carrots, turnips, radishes, and beets have an extended growing period during the winter, allowing them to develop into hearty and flavorful crops. The colder temperatures encourage the growth of vibrant and crisp root vegetables, enhancing the culinary experience and offering a delightful variety to winter dishes. By sowing these seeds in the fall, gardeners can reap the rewards of their patience and dedication as they harvest these delicious vegetables throughout the winter months.

While we primarily focus on edible crops, it's worth noting that winter gardens can also incorporate beautiful and hardy flowers. These flowers not only add aesthetic appeal to outdoor spaces but also bring a sense of vibrancy and life to an otherwise dormant landscape. Hardy winter flowers, such as pansies, cyclamen, and winter jasmine, thrive in cooler temperatures and can withstand frost and snow. By including these resilient blooms in your winter garden, you can create a visual oasis amid the winter chill and enjoy their captivating colors and fragrances.

HOW TO COVER A RAISED BED FOR CONTINUED GROWTH

When it comes to optimizing plant growth and safeguarding your raised beds, covering them becomes essential. In this section, we will delve into various types of covers that can be employed to shield raised beds, ensuring continued growth and protection despite changing weather conditions. We will discuss hoop houses, box frame covers, retractable covers, cold frames, pop-up or fixed cloches, and plant tents, providing specific insights into their benefits and step-by-step instructions on how to use them effectively in your garden.

Hoop Houses:

1. Construct a series of arches using PVC pipes or metal hoops anchored on either side of the raised bed.
2. Drape a translucent covering material, such as greenhouse plastic or row cover fabric, over the arches, ensuring it is securely fastened.
3. Adjust the height and tension of the covering material to provide adequate space for plant growth.
4. To keep it from being blown away by wind or other forces, fasten the ends of the covering cloth.

Box Frame Covers:

1. Build a frame using wood or PVC pipes that fit directly over the raised bed, ensuring it is sturdy and well anchored.
2. Cover the frame with a transparent material like greenhouse plastic or clear polyethylene.
3. Ensure the cover extends to the sides and reaches the ground, sealing the raised bed completely.
4. Include hinged or removable panels in the cover design for easy access to the plants when watering, harvesting, or performing maintenance.

Retractable Covers:

1. Construct a lightweight frame using PVC or metal, sized to fit the dimensions of your raised bed.
2. Attach a removable plastic or fabric material to the frame.
3. Install a mechanism that allows the cover to be easily adjusted in height, accommodating plants of different sizes as they grow.
4. To guard against being blown away by wind or other outside forces, tightly fasten the cover to the frame.

Cold Frames:

1. Build a solid frame using wood or metal that matches the size of the raised bed.
2. Attach transparent panels, such as glass or polycarbonate, to create the sloping structure of the cold frame.
3. Place the cold frame over the raised bed, ensuring it is firmly positioned and level.
4. Ventilate the cold frame during the day to prevent overheating and close it at night to retain heat and protect plants from frost.

Pop-up/Fixed Cloches:

1. Select a suitable cloche material, such as plastic, glass, or repurposed containers like plastic bottles.
2. Position the cloche directly over the desired plant or a smaller section of the raised bed.
3. Secure the cloche in place, ensuring it is firmly anchored to prevent it from being displaced by wind or other elements.
4. Monitor the temperature inside the cloche and adjust ventilation as needed to prevent excessive heat buildup.

Plant Tents:

1. Assemble a lightweight frame for the plant tent using materials like PVC or metal.
2. Cover the frame with a removable, transparent material such as greenhouse plastic or clear polyethylene.
3. Set up the plant tent over the raised bed, ensuring it covers the entire area and is securely anchored.
4. Adjust the height and tension of the cover as necessary, allowing ample space for plant growth and ventilation.

By following these step-by-step instructions for each type of cover, you can effectively shield your raised beds and provide optimal conditions for your plants to grow and thrive, regardless of the weather conditions outside.

GROW COVER CROPS

Your raised beds' health and output are greatly enhanced by cover crops. They not only protect the soil but also provide a range of benefits, such as adding organic matter, reducing nematodes, suppressing diseases, improving airflow, adding nutrients, reducing weeds, and providing food for pollinators. In this section, we will explore the best winter cover crops for raised beds and provide a summary of each, along with step-by-step instructions on how to grow them effectively.

Step 1: Choose the Right Winter Cover Crop.

- Consider the specific needs of your garden, such as soil type, climate, and desired benefits.
- Common winter cover crops for raised beds include crimson clover, hairy vetch, winter rye, Austrian winter peas, and winter wheat.

Step 2: Prepare the Raised Bed.

- Clear the raised bed of any existing plants and debris.
- Remove weeds or unwanted vegetation from the bed.

Step 3: Sow the Cover Crop Seeds.

- Follow the recommended seeding rate provided on the cover crop seed packet.
- Broadcast the seeds evenly over the raised bed.
- Rake the ground lightly to scatter some soil or compost over the seeds.

Step 4: Water and Maintain.

- Water the raised bed thoroughly after sowing the cover crop seeds.

- Maintain consistent moisture levels throughout the germination and growth stages.
- Monitor the cover crop for any signs of stress or disease and take appropriate action if needed.

Step 5: Give the Cover Crop Space to Expand.

- Give the cover crop the necessary amount of time to grow, usually until it reaches the flowering or seed-setting stage.
- The cover crop choice and the local climate can affect this growing period.

Step 6: Incorporate the Cover Crop.

- Cut the cover crop back using garden shears or a lawn mower.
- Allow the cut cover crop to remain on the soil surface as a mulch or incorporate it into the soil as green manure.
- If incorporating, use a garden fork or tiller to mix the cover crop residues into the top layer of soil.

Step 7: Repeat the Process.

- After incorporating the cover crop, prepare the raised bed for the next planting cycle.

- Repeat the cover cropping process in subsequent seasons or as needed to continually improve soil health and fertility.

Best Winter Cover Crops for Raised Beds:

Crimson Clover:

- Fast-growing nitrogen-fixing legume.
- Early fall or late summer are good times to sow.
- Incorporate before flowering or allow it to self-seed.

Hairy Vetch:

- Hardy nitrogen-fixing legume.
- Sow in the late summer or early fall.
- Cut back before flowering or in early spring.

Austrian Winter Peas:

- Nitrogen-fixing legume.
- Sow in the late summer or early fall.
- Cut back before flowering or in early spring.

Winter Wheat:

- Cereal grain.
- Sow in the late summer or early fall.

- Cut it back before it goes to seed or in the early spring.

By following these step-by-step instructions and choosing the appropriate winter cover crops for your raised beds, you can improve soil health, suppress weeds, enrich nutrient content, and create an ecosystem that supports pollinators. Cover crops are a valuable tool for maximizing the productivity and sustainability of your garden, ensuring long-term success and abundance.

VIBRANT WINTER BERRIES FOR RAISED BEDS

Your garden doesn't have to be drab and lifeless during the winter. In fact, it can be a time of vibrant colors and delightful surprises, especially when you incorporate plants that bear stunning winter berries into your raised beds. These berries not only add visual interest but also attract birds and other wildlife, creating a lively and dynamic garden ecosystem. In this section, we will explore a range of enchanting winter berries that are perfect for raised beds, providing an overview of each, and inspiring you to infuse your garden with their beauty.

Callicarpa bodinieri:

- Commonly known as beautyberry.
- Showcases clusters of vibrant purple berries.
- Gives your winter landscape a splash of color.

Gaultheria procumbens:

- Also called wintergreen or checkerberry.
- Features glossy, round red berries.
- Offers a fresh, minty fragrance and evergreen foliage.

Spindle Tree (Euonymus):

- Boasts unique spindle-shaped fruits in vibrant shades of pink, orange, or red.
- Adds a whimsical touch to your garden.

Holly (Ilex):

- Iconic evergreen shrub with red, yellow, or orange berries.
- Perfect for festive holiday decorations.

Snowberry (Symphoricarpos):

- Produces delicate clusters of white berries.
- Creates a graceful and ethereal look in winter.

Aucuba japonica:

- Features glossy, speckled leaves and vibrant red berries.

- Thrives in shady areas, adding color to dimly lit corners.

Viburnum:

- Offers a variety of species with different berry colors, including red, blue, and black.
- Delights with fragrant flowers in spring and berries that last into winter.

Mistletoe (Viscum album):

- A traditional symbol of love and celebration.
- Bears white berries and adds a touch of magic to your garden.

Pyracantha coccinea:

- Known as firethorn.
- Bright clusters of red, orange, or yellow berries will adorn your raised beds.
- Serves as a natural barrier due to its thorny branches.

Rose Hips:

- Result from the pollinated flowers of roses.

- Offer a range of colors, from vibrant red to deep orange.
- Ensure that birds have a reliable source of food during the winter.

Hawthorn (Crataegus):

- Displays clusters of red or orange berries.
- Attracts birds and adds a rustic charm to your garden.

Pink Pagoda (Itea virginica):

- Showcases pinkish-white flowers in summer, followed by clusters of pink berries.
- Provides a striking contrast against its dark green foliage.

Rowan (Sorbus):

- Bears clusters of small red or orange berries.
- Gives your raised beds a splash of natural splendor.

Cotoneaster:

- Offers a range of species with colorful berries, such as red, orange, or black.
- Adds a vibrant display to your winter garden.

Skimmia Japonica 'Humpty Dumpty':

- Features compact growth and clusters of bright red berries.
- Perfect for smaller raised beds or containers.

By incorporating these stunning winter berry plants into your raised beds, you can create a vibrant and visually captivating garden even during the coldest months. These berries not only improve your garden's appearance but also increase its biodiversity by giving birds a nutritious food source. Embrace the beauty of winter and let these captivating berries transform your raised beds into a winter wonderland.

Interactive Element

To help you visually plan and keep track of maintaining your raised beds in winter, we have created an interactive timeline. The duties and plantings you should think about throughout this season are clearly outlined in this timeline. It also reminds you to add a layer of mulch to protect your plants and promote healthy growth.

Winter Raised Bed Maintenance Timeline:

Late Fall (November):

- Clean up any debris and remove spent annual plants.
- Cut back perennial plants and remove any diseased foliage.
- To shield the soil from changes in temperature, add a layer of organic mulch.

Early Winter (December):

- Grow cold-tolerant plants like Swiss chard, kale, lettuce, and spinach.
- Cover your raised beds with row covers or cloches to provide extra protection from frost.

Mid-Winter (January):

- Check your raised beds for pest or disease indicators and take the necessary action.
- Check moisture levels in the soil and water as needed.
- Consider adding winter cover crops to enrich the soil and prevent erosion.

Late Winter (February):

- Start preparing for the upcoming growing season by planning your crop rotation and ordering seeds.
- Prune any fruit trees or berry bushes that require winter pruning.

Remember to add your own notes and observations throughout the timeline. This will help you keep track of specific observations, such as pest sightings, growth progress, or any additional tasks that are unique to your garden.

Pests are a natural part of every garden, and it's important to understand that not all pests are bad. In the penultimate chapter, we will see how to use certain plants to attract beneficial insects and those plants that will deter the not-so-beneficial ones.

8

PAIRING PLANTS TO PREVENT PESTS

In the world of gardening, pests can often pose a significant challenge. These unwelcome visitors can wreak havoc on our plants, leaving us frustrated and searching for effective solutions. But what if I told you that there's a natural way to prevent pests and promote the overall health of your plants? It's called companion planting, and in this chapter, we will explore its remarkable benefits.

Companion planting goes beyond traditional pest control methods. It involves strategically pairing plants that work together harmoniously, not only deterring pests but also enhancing flavor and improving plant vitality. By understanding the principles of companion planting, you can create a thriving garden ecosystem where plants support and protect each other.

In this chapter, we will delve into the fascinating world of pairing plants to prevent pests. We will explore how certain plants can repel or confuse pests, acting as natural deterrents. Additionally, we will discover the importance of attracting beneficial insects, such as wasps, to our gardens. Contrary to popular belief, wasps play a vital role in pollination and serve as valuable allies in controlling less desirable garden pests.

By the end of this chapter, you will not only be able to identify the signs of pest infestations but also possess the knowledge to effectively manage them through natural means. You will learn which plants attract beneficial insects, creating a balanced ecosystem that promotes plant health and reduces the need for harmful chemicals.

So, let's jump right in to uncover the secrets of companion planting and embrace a more sustainable and pest-resistant garden. Get ready to discover the power of pairing plants to prevent pests and unlock a world of natural beauty and abundance.

WHAT IS COMPANION PLANTING?

Companion planting is a fascinating technique that unlocks the hidden potential of our gardens. It involves strategically pairing specific plants together to create a harmonious environment where they can support and benefit one another. While companion planting offers numerous advantages beyond pest control, it is also the foundation for a thriving and sustainable garden. In this section, we will explore the benefits of companion planting, highlight the Native American practice of the Three Sisters, and list the steps involved in implementing this technique.

Understanding the Benefits of Companion Planting

Companion planting extends far beyond the realm of pest control. It uses the strength of plant interactions to raise soil fertility, promote plant development, and boost agricultural yields. By carefully selecting compatible plants, we can create a dynamic ecosystem where each species fulfills a unique role. The key benefits include the following:

- **Pest Management:** Certain plants act as natural repellents, masking the scent of more desirable plants and deterring pests. Marigolds, for instance, deter worms, while basil wards off insects.
- **Nutrient Cycling:** Companion plants with varying root depths and nutrient requirements can complement each other, ensuring efficient utilization of soil nutrients and reducing competition.
- **Pollination and Beneficial Insects:** Some plants attract pollinators and beneficial insects, which aid in the fertilization of flowers and act as natural predators against garden pests. The presence of

flowering herbs, such as lavender and dill, can attract bees and ladybugs.

- **Weed Suppression:** Companion plants with dense foliage can suppress weed growth by blocking sunlight and limiting available resources for weeds.
- **Improved Flavor and Productivity:** Certain plant combinations enhance the flavor of neighboring crops and even increase their productivity. This phenomenon is known as "flavor synergy" and can be observed in combinations like tomatoes and basil.

The Three Sisters: A Native American Example of Companion Planting

One remarkable example of companion planting is the Native American practice known as the Three Sisters. Corn, beans, and squash are interplanted in this age-old method. Each plant provides unique benefits to the others:

- **Corn**: The tall cornstalks serve as a natural trellis for the climbing beans, allowing them to reach greater heights and maximize sunlight exposure.
- **Beans**: The bean plants fix nitrogen into the soil, providing a natural fertilizer for corn and squash. Additionally, their vining nature helps stabilize the corn plants against strong winds.
- **Squash**: The large, sprawling squash leaves create a natural mulch, suppressing weed growth, retaining

soil moisture, and providing shade, which helps prevent evaporation and keep the soil cool.

Steps for Implementing Companion Planting

Implementing companion planting in your own garden is an exciting endeavor that requires careful planning and consideration. Here are the steps to get started:

1. **Research and Select Compatible Plants:** Familiarize yourself with the characteristics, needs, and interactions of different plant species. Determine the plants that can cooperate and profit from being planted close to one another.
2. **Design Your Garden Layout:** Consider factors such as plant heights, sunlight requirements, and space availability when arranging your companion plants. Aim for a balanced and visually appealing garden layout.
3. **Rotate Crops:** Rotate your crops to prevent the accumulation of pests and illnesses. Refrain from consistently growing the same crop in the same place.
4. **Monitor and Adapt:** Regularly observe your garden for signs of pests, diseases, or imbalances. If necessary, alter your companion planting techniques to keep your garden flourishing and fruitful.

By embracing the principles of companion planting, you can create a thriving and sustainable garden ecosystem. The practice not only helps control pests but also improves pollination, enhances soil fertility, and promotes the overall health and productivity of plants.

RECOGNIZING PEST INFESTATIONS

Maintaining a thriving garden is a labor of love, but it often comes with its fair share of challenges. Dealing with pest infestations that can cause havoc on our plants is one of these difficulties. To effectively combat these unwanted visitors, it is crucial to be able to recognize and identify the specific pests causing the damage. In this section, we will explore how to identify garden pests by their physical characteristics, the types of damage they inflict, and the specific host plants they tend to target.

Identifying Garden Pests by Physical Description

A crucial first step in recognizing pest infestations is being able to identify the culprits by their physical characteristics. By familiarizing yourself with the appearance of common garden pests, you can quickly assess the situation and take appropriate measures. Observe the following important physical characteristics:

- **Insects**: Observe the size, shape, color, and patterns of insects. For example, aphids are small, soft-bodied insects that come in various colors, while caterpillars have a segmented body and multiple legs.
- **Snails and Slugs**: They move by sliding along a slime path, and these mollusks have soft bodies. They frequently have a grayish or brown appearance.
- **Rodents**: Rats and mice have distinct long tails and large front incisor teeth. They leave behind gnaw marks and droppings as evidence of their presence.

Types of Damage Caused by Garden Pests

Garden pests can cause a range of damage to plants, including:

- **Chewing Damage**: Pests such as caterpillars, beetles, and grasshoppers feed on plant leaves, resulting in irregular holes or chewed edges.
- **Sucking Damage**: Insects like aphids and mites extract sap from plants, causing leaves to wilt, turn yellow, or become distorted.
- **Tunneling Damage**: Larvae of pests like borers and root maggots tunnel into stems or roots, leading to weakened plants, stunted growth, and even plant death.
- **Fruit and Flower Damage**: Pests like fruit flies and thrips can cause damage to fruits and flowers,

resulting in blemishes, premature dropping, or deformation.

Identifying Pest Infestations by Host Plants

Certain pests have a strong preference for specific host plants. By understanding their plant preferences, you can quickly identify potential infestations. Some examples include:

- **Tomato Hornworm**: These large green caterpillars with horn-like structures are commonly found on tomato plants, feeding voraciously on the foliage.
- **Cabbage White Butterfly**: The adult butterfly lays eggs on cabbage family plants, and the resulting caterpillars feed on the leaves, often leaving behind a characteristic Swiss cheese-like pattern.
- **Japanese Beetle**: These metallic green beetles consume a broad variety of plants, such as fruit trees, roses, and grapes, leaving behind skeletonized leaves in their wake.
- **Aphids**: These tiny, soft-bodied insects often gather on new growth, sucking sap from the plant. They can be found on a wide range of plants, including ornamentals, vegetables, and roses.

By being attentive to the specific plants that pests target, you can focus your pest management efforts and take proactive measures to protect susceptible plants.

HOW TO PAIR PLANTS FOR PEST CONTROL

In the pursuit of a pest-free garden, it's important to explore sustainable and eco-friendly methods. One such method is companion planting for pest control, which involves strategically pairing specific plants together to deter pests naturally.

Steps 1 through 16 will be used to walk you through the process of matching plants for efficient pest management in this section. By implementing these strategies, you can create a balanced and harmonious garden ecosystem that naturally repels pests while promoting plant health and vitality.

1. **Understand Companion Planting.** Plants that interact favorably with one another are paired together in a process known as companion planting. By carefully selecting plant combinations, you can enhance pest control, improve soil health, and increase crop productivity.

2. **Research Pest-Repelling Plants.** Identify plants that are known for their pest-repellent properties. For example, marigolds emit a scent that deters aphids, nematodes, and other pests. By including these plants in your garden, you can make a secure perimeter against trespassers.

3. **Attract Beneficial Insects.** Some plants draw advantageous insects that feed on garden pests. For instance, planting dill, fennel, or yarrow can lure ladybugs, lacewings, and praying mantises, which feed on aphids and other common pests.

4. **Create Plant Diversity.** Promote plant diversity in your garden to prevent the buildup of specific pest populations. Different plants attract different pests, so by having a variety of species, you can minimize the impact of any single pest.

5. **Interplant Pest-Repelling Herbs.** Plant herbs with natural pest-repellent properties alongside susceptible crops. Basil, for instance, can deter tomato hornworms and aphids when grown near tomatoes. Similarly, rosemary and sage can repel pests like cabbage moths when planted alongside brassicas.

6. **Establish Aromatic Barriers.** Use aromatic plants to create barriers that repel pests. Garlic, chives, and onions, for example, emit strong odors that deter aphids, slugs, and carrot flies. By planting them strategically, you can protect vulnerable crops.

7. **Employ Trap Crops.** Strategically plant trap crops to divert pests away from your main crops. Radishes or nasturtiums, for instance, can attract flea beetles and aphids, keeping them away from your desired plants.

8. **Follow the Three Sisters Method.** Adopt the Native American technique known as the Three Sisters

method. By planting corn, beans, and squash together, you create a symbiotic system where each plant benefits the others, providing shade, support, and deterring pests.

9. **Rotate Crops.** Rotate your crops to disrupt the life cycles of pests. Recurring planting of the same crop or closely related plants in the same location might encourage the establishment and growth of pests. Rotate crops to prevent infestations.

10. **Incorporate Beneficial Flowers.** Incorporate beneficial flowers that not only add beauty to your garden but also attract pollinators and natural predators of pests. Sunflowers, zinnias, and calendula, for example, attract bees and other pollinators while deterring pests like aphids and spider mites.

11. **Provide Physical Barriers.** To keep pests away from sensitive plants, use physical barriers like row covers or netting. These barriers can prevent insects from reaching your crops, effectively reducing the risk of infestation.

12. **Practice Intercropping.** Intercrop plants with different growth habits to maximize space and discourage pests. For instance, tall plants like corn can provide shade and support for shorter plants like cucumbers, while also interfering with the flight patterns of pests.

13. **Companion Plant With Alliums.** Alliums, including garlic, onions, and leeks, have natural pest-repelling properties. By interplanting them with susceptible crops, you can deter pests like aphids, carrot flies, and cabbage worms.

14. **Combine Pest-Repelling Herbs.** Create herb combinations that work together to deter pests. For example, planting thyme and mint near each other can repel pests like cabbage worms and ants.

15. **Consider Succession Planting.** Implement succession planting to minimize the impact of pests. By staggering the planting of crops, you can avoid having a large number of susceptible plants at the same time, reducing the likelihood of widespread infestation.

16. **Regular Monitoring and Maintenance.** Continuously monitor your garden for signs of pests and take immediate action when necessary. Regularly inspect plants for damage, look for pests or their eggs, and remove any affected foliage or insects manually.

By following these steps and implementing companion planting strategies, you can create a garden that naturally deters pests and promotes the health and vitality of your plants. Remember to choose the right companion plants based on their pest-repelling properties and specific crop needs.

HOMEMADE SOLUTIONS FOR PESTS

When it comes to dealing with pests in and around your home, you don't always have to rely on chemical-laden products. There are plenty of natural and homemade solutions that can effectively help control pests without harming the environment or your health. In this section, we will explore some of these homemade solutions and how they can be used to tackle common pest problems.

Coffee Grounds: Coffee grounds may be used to ward off bugs … did you know that? To keep pests like ants, slugs, and snails away from your garden beds or potted plants, scatter nitrogen-rich coffee grounds around the area. These pests dislike the strong scent of coffee and will avoid areas treated with coffee grounds. Additionally, coffee grounds can act as a natural fertilizer, providing nutrients to your plants as they break down.

Banana Skins: Before tossing those banana skins in the trash, consider using them to ward off pests. Banana skins contain compounds like potassium and phosphorus that can help strengthen plants and make them more resistant to pests. Peels from bananas should be chopped up and buried in the soil close to your plants. This can help deter aphids, spider mites, and other common garden pests.

Apple Cider Vinegar: Pest management is just one of the many uses for apple cider vinegar, which is a multifunctional substance. It works as a trap because pests like fruit flies and gnats are drawn to its potent scent. Fill a small container with apple cider vinegar and a few drops of dish soap to make a straightforward apple cider vinegar trap. Although the dish soap will break the surface tension and drown the pests, the vinegar will attract them.

Cornmeal: Cornmeal can be used as a natural pesticide for controlling pests like ants and cockroaches. Cornmeal causes ants to die when they eat it because it swells in their digestive tract. If you see ant trails or cockroach activity, scatter cornmeal there. Over time, the pests will be successfully eliminated since they will bring the cornmeal back to their nests.

White Vinegar: White vinegar is another common household ingredient that can be used for pest control. Ants, spiders, and other insects can be repelled with the help of its potent acidic characteristics. A homemade insect repellent spray can be prepared by combining white vinegar and water in equal parts. In locations where pests are prone to infiltrate your home, such as cracks and access points, apply this solution with a spray bottle.

Onions: Onions have natural insect-repellent properties, making them a useful tool in pest control. By mixing a few onions with water and draining the product, you may make your own onion spray. The resulting liquid can be sprayed on plants to repel pests like aphids and caterpillars. It's important to reapply the spray regularly, especially after rain or watering, to maintain its effectiveness.

Cloves: The strong scent of cloves can also help in deterring pests. Cloves are known to repel insects like mosquitoes, flies, and ants. You can create a simple homemade clove repellent by placing whole cloves in a small sachet or tying them up in a piece of cheesecloth. Hang these sachets or place them strategically around your home or garden to keep pests at bay.

These homemade solutions offer a natural and eco-friendly approach to pest control. They are safer alternatives to chemical pesticides and can be easily made with ingredients commonly found in your kitchen or pantry. By utilizing these homemade remedies, you not only protect your plants and home from pests but also promote a healthier and more sustainable environment.

Interactive Element

The companion plants, their allies, and their enemies are shown in the straightforward and quick-to-read chart below. You may plan your garden and choose the best plant combinations for optimum development and pest management with the help of this interactive chart.

PLANTS	FRIENDS	FOES
Tomatoes	Basil, Marigold	Cabbage, Corn
Carrots	Chives, Onions	Dill, Parsley
Lettuce	Carrots, Radishes	Cabbage, Parsley
Cucumbers	Beans, Corn	Potatoes, Aromatic Herbs
Beans	Carrots, Cucumbers	Onions, Garlic
Peppers	Basil, Marigold	Fennel, Kohlrabi
Onions	Beets, Carrots	Peas, Beans
Spinach	Strawberries	Potatoes, Cabbage
Broccoli	Chamomile, Dill	Tomatoes, Grapes

The compatibility of typical companion plants is quickly summarized in this chart. You may improve your garden's growth, flavor, and general health while preventing pests and boosting pollination by planting specific combinations.

In the final chapter, we will look at the final P in the method and what to do when plants need protection from disease.

9

PROTECTING PLANTS FROM DISEASE

In this chapter, we will focus on identifying some different plant diseases and explore homemade, natural solutions to effectively treat them. Additionally, we will conclude with essential maintenance tips and practices that can significantly reduce the risk of plant diseases.

To comprehend the dynamics of plant diseases, we must first grasp the concept of the disease triangle. It consists of three key components: the host (the plant itself), the pathogen (the microorganism responsible for causing the disease, such as fungi or bacteria), and a susceptible environment. By understanding this triangle, we can take proactive steps to ensure our raised beds are not conducive to disease development.

It is crucial to create an environment in your raised beds that minimizes the likelihood of diseases taking hold. By implementing appropriate practices and being mindful of the factors that attract diseases, you can effectively safeguard your plants' health and vitality.

Throughout this chapter, we will explore a comprehensive guide to identifying various plant diseases, including the physical symptoms and signs to watch for. With this information at your disposal, you will be more prepared to act quickly and stop the spread of diseases.

Moreover, we will also discuss natural and homemade remedies to treat plant diseases. By harnessing the power of organic solutions such as herbal extracts, compost teas, and biofungicides, you can combat diseases while minimizing the use of synthetic chemicals.

Lastly, we will emphasize the importance of regular maintenance and good gardening practices to reduce the risk of diseases. Proper sanitation, crop rotation, adequate watering, and promoting a healthy soil ecosystem are just a few of the essential techniques we will explore.

By the end of this chapter, you will have gained valuable insights into identifying plant diseases, using natural treatment options, and adopting preventive measures. Armed with this knowledge, you can cultivate a thriving garden that is resilient against diseases, ensuring the health and longevity of your plants.

HOW TO REDUCE THE RISK OF DISEASED PLANTS

To cultivate a healthy and vibrant garden, it is crucial to prioritize disease prevention. By implementing effective strategies and practices, you can significantly reduce the risk of plant diseases and promote the overall well-being of your plants. In this section, we will explore key steps to mitigate the risk of diseased plants and create an environment where they can thrive.

Building on What We Have Learned

Let's begin by revisiting the valuable lessons we have learned so far, such as proper watering, mulching, pruning, and feeding. These practices help maintain optimal plant health, strengthen their immune systems, and create conditions that are less favorable for disease development. By consistently applying these techniques, you are taking proactive steps toward reducing the risk of diseases in your garden.

Starting With the Right Soil

An essential aspect of disease prevention is starting with healthy soil. A nutrient-rich and well-drained soil creates an optimal foundation for plants to grow strong and resilient. You can create an environment where plants are less susceptible to illnesses by enriching the soil with organic materials, such as compost, and ensuring good drainage. Healthy soil supports robust root systems and enables plants to withstand potential threats.

Additionally, consider conducting soil tests to assess nutrient levels and pH. Adjusting the soil's pH to suit specific plants' requirements can promote their vitality and disease resistance. Incorporating beneficial soil microbes and organisms through organic amendments also enhances the soil's overall health and resilience.

Disease-Resistant Plants

Incorporating disease-resistant plants into your raised beds is another effective strategy to minimize the risk of disease. These plants possess inherent genetic traits that make them less susceptible to common diseases prevalent in your region. Research and select varieties known for their resistance to specific diseases, such as powdery mildew, fungal infections, or viral diseases.

Consult local nurseries, gardening experts, or extension services for recommendations on disease-resistant plants that thrive in your area. By integrating these plants into your garden, you create a natural defense against potential disease outbreaks, reducing the need for extensive intervention or chemical treatments.

By adopting these measures and incorporating disease-resistant plants, you are taking proactive steps to minimize the risk of diseases in your raised beds. However, it is important to remain vigilant and monitor your plants regularly for any signs of distress or disease symptoms. The spread of diseases and the preservation of your garden's general health can both be achieved through early identification and prompt response.

6 COMMON PLANT DISEASES

As gardeners, it is important to be familiar with common plant diseases in order to protect our plants and ensure their health. In this section, I will discuss six common plant diseases: leaf spots, mosaic virus, powdery mildew, rust, gray and black mold, and dampening off. By understanding their characteristics and learning how to identify them, you can take proactive measures to prevent and manage these diseases, ensuring the well-being of your plants.

1. **Leaf Spots:** Leaf spots are caused by fungal or bacterial infections and appear as small, discolored lesions on plant leaves. To identify leaf spots, closely examine the leaves for circular or irregular browning, yellowing, or blackening. Fungal leaf spots may have a fuzzy or powdery appearance. Promptly remove infected leaves and maintain good air circulation to control the spread of leaf spots.

2. **Mosaic Virus:** The mosaic virus is a viral infection that results in distinct mosaic-like patterns on plant leaves. Look for mottled or streaked discoloration,

distorted growth, and reduced plant vigor as signs of mosaic virus. Since there is no treatment for this illness, prevention is essential. Use disease-free seeds or transplants and practice strict sanitation measures to minimize the risk of mosaic virus.

3. **Powdery Mildew:** Powdery mildew is a fungal disease characterized by a white or grayish powdery coating on leaves, stems, and flowers. Leaves may also curl or distort. Proper identification of powdery mildew includes observing the distinctive powdery growth. Control powdery mildew by providing adequate air circulation, avoiding overhead watering, and applying fungicidal treatments when necessary.

4. **Rust:** Rust is a fungal disease that manifests as orange, yellow, or brown pustules on the undersides of leaves, stems, or fruits. It leads to leaf yellowing, premature defoliation, and weakened plant vigor. Rust spreads through airborne spores and thrives in warm and humid conditions. Manage rust by promptly removing infected plant parts and ensuring good air circulation.

5. **Gray and Black Mold:** Gray and black molds are common fungal infections that develop in damp and humid conditions. They appear as fuzzy or powdery growth on leaves, flowers, or fruits. These molds can hinder photosynthesis and cause tissue decay. Control gray and black molds by improving air

circulation, practicing proper watering techniques, and removing affected plant parts.

6. **Dampening Off:** Dampening off is a fungal disease that primarily affects young seedlings. It causes sudden collapse, wilting, and the death of seedlings, often at the soil level. Look for dark-colored lesions or a water-soaked appearance in infected seedlings. Prevent dampening by using sterilized soil or growing media, avoiding overwatering, ensuring proper drainage, and maintaining clean gardening tools.

TREATING PLANT DISEASES

When faced with plant diseases, it is crucial to take immediate action to prevent their spread and protect the health of your garden. In this section, we will look at effective organic treatments for common plant diseases. By understanding the benefits and application methods of natural remedies such as apple cider vinegar, baking soda, hydrogen peroxide, milk, and neem oil, you can combat plant diseases while maintaining an eco-friendly approach.

- **Apple Cider Vinegar:** Due to its antifungal and antibacterial qualities, apple cider vinegar is useful in the treatment of a variety of plant diseases. Three parts water and one part apple cider vinegar should be combined to create a solution. Spray this solution onto the affected plants, ensuring thorough coverage. Apple cider vinegar helps control fungal infections, such as powdery mildew, by altering the pH and creating an unfavorable environment for pathogens.

- **Baking Soda:** Baking soda is a versatile ingredient that can be used to treat fungal diseases, including powdery mildew and black spot. Mix one teaspoon of mild liquid soap, one tablespoon of baking soda, and one gallon of water to make a solution. Stir the mixture thoroughly before applying it to the harmed plants. The pH is changed with baking soda, which also prevents fungus from growing.

- **Hydrogen Peroxide:** Hydrogen peroxide is an oxygen-rich compound that aids in plant health and fights against diseases caused by anaerobic pathogens. Apply the solution to the afflicted plants with a spray bottle after combining one part hydrogen peroxide with three parts water. Hydrogen peroxide helps control diseases like root rot and bacterial infections by providing oxygen and promoting a healthy root environment.

- **Milk:** Milk has been found to have antifungal properties, particularly against powdery mildew. Create a mixture by diluting one part milk with two parts water. Make sure the afflicted plants are completely covered by the solution when spraying it on the plants. The proteins in milk help suppress the growth of powdery mildew and boost the plant's natural defense mechanisms.

- **Neem Oil:** The neem tree produces neem oil, which has broad-spectrum fungicidal and insecticidal effects. To make a neem oil solution, mix one teaspoon of neem oil with one quart of water and add a few drops of mild liquid soap to enhance the emulsification. Spray the remedy liberally over the afflicted plants, being sure to cover both leaf surfaces. Neem oil disrupts the life cycle of pests and pathogens, controlling diseases like black spot and rust.

Organic treatment of plant diseases is a successful and environmentally responsible strategy. By using apple cider vinegar, baking soda, hydrogen peroxide, milk, and neem oil, you can combat common plant diseases and promote a healthy garden.

KEEPING GARDENS CLEAN

A tidy garden not only improves its aesthetic appeal but is essential to the general well-being and productivity of plants. This section will discuss the importance of maintaining cleanliness in gardens and offer helpful advice for doing so.

- **Clearing Debris and Diseased Plants:** One of the fundamental steps in keeping gardens clean is regularly clearing debris and removing diseased plants. Fallen leaves, dead plant material, and other organic debris can harbor pests, fungi, and pathogens, providing a breeding ground for diseases. By promptly removing this debris, you minimize the risk of diseases spreading and infesting healthy plants.

- **Cleaning Garden Tools:** Garden tools can inadvertently carry pathogens and diseases from one plant to another if not properly cleaned. After using tools on infected plants, it is crucial to clean and disinfect them to prevent cross-contamination. The use of a bleach solution is advised for cleaning garden implements. The tools should be soaked for ten to fifteen minutes in a solution of one part bleach to nine parts water. Rinse them off well, scrub away any lingering grime, and then let them air dry.

- **Treating Wooden Handles:** Wooden handles on garden tools are prone to splitting and cracking due to exposure to moisture and weathering. To ensure their longevity and prevent potential damage, it is advisable to treat wooden handles with a plant-based oil. Apply linseed oil or any other suitable plant-based oil to the handles, following the manufacturer's instructions. This treatment helps nourish and protect the wood, keeping the handles in good condition.

- **Regular Maintenance:** In addition to specific cleaning tasks, regular maintenance of the garden is essential for cleanliness. This includes routine weeding, removing spent flowers, and pruning to maintain the overall health and appearance of plants.

Maintaining cleanliness in the garden is vital for promoting the health and vitality of your plants.

Interactive Element

Use this checklist to ensure you're implementing best practices and keeping your garden in optimal condition:

- **Clear debris**: Remove fallen leaves, dead plants, and any other organic debris from the raised beds regularly to prevent pests and diseases.
- **Weed control**: Keep weeds in check by regularly inspecting the raised beds and removing any unwanted plants. This will prevent competition for nutrients and resources.
- **Watering**: Monitor soil moisture levels and water the raised beds as needed. Ensure that the plants receive enough water but refrain from overwatering to prevent root rot and other problems.

- **Mulching**: Around the plants in the raised beds, spread a layer of organic mulch made of straw or wood chips. Mulching aids in moisture retention, controls weed growth, and maintains soil temperature.
- **Pruning**: Prune plants as necessary to remove dead or diseased branches, improve airflow, and promote healthy growth. To prevent the plants from being harmed, use tidy, sharp pruning tools.
- **Fertilization**: Provide nutrients to your plants by applying organic fertilizers or compost to the raised beds. Avoid overfertilizing, which can harm the plants, by adhering to the suggested application rates.
- **Pest control**: Regularly check the raised beds for pests and take the necessary precautions to control them. This can include handpicking pests, using natural pest repellents, or employing companion planting techniques.
- **Disease prevention**: Implement preventive measures to minimize the risk of diseases. These include proper plant spacing, ensuring good airflow, and avoiding overhead watering that can promote fungal infections.
- **Soil testing**: Periodically test the soil in your raised beds to assess nutrient levels and pH. Based on the test results, make the necessary adjustments by

adding soil amendments or adjusting fertilizer applications.

- **Crop rotation**: Each season, rotate the crops in the raised beds to prevent the accumulation of pests and diseases that attack particular plant groups.

- **Tool maintenance**: To stop the transmission of disease, disinfect and clean gardening equipment after each use. Regularly sharpen cutting tools and oil wooden handles to keep them in good condition.

- **Harvest regularly**: Harvest mature fruits, vegetables, and herbs promptly to maintain plant health and encourage continuous production.

- **Monitor for signs of stress:** Check your plants frequently for any indications of stress, like discoloration, wilting, or odd growth patterns. Adapt your watering strategy or deal with nutrient deficits as necessary.

- **Composting**: Utilize a composting system to recycle garden waste and kitchen scraps. Compost can be added to the raised beds as a nutrient-rich amendment.

- **Record keeping**: Maintain a garden journal to track planting dates, crop performance, pest and disease issues, and any specific observations or interventions. This information will help you make informed decisions and plan for future seasons.

Remember, each garden is unique, and specific maintenance needs may vary. Adjust this checklist based on your garden's specific requirements and the plants you are growing.

THE 7TH P

Remember that bonus 7th P? This is your chance to pass on your new knowledge – with barely any effort at all!

Simply by sharing your honest opinion of this book and a little about your own journey into gardening, you'll show new readers where they can find everything they need to get started with raised bed gardening.

Thank you so much for your support. I wish you many abundant harvests.

Scan the QR code to leave your review!

CONCLUSION

You now have an all-inclusive guide for productive raised bed gardening thanks to this book. Throughout the chapters, we have explored the numerous benefits of raised beds and how they offer a wide range of options to create a thriving garden without breaking the bank. Let's recap the key takeaways and reinforce the 6 Ps that will ensure your raised bed gardening journey is a resounding success.

First and foremost, proper **planning** is crucial. Take the time to assess your space, evaluate the amount of sunlight it receives, and consider the specific needs and preferences of the plants you want to grow. By planning ahead, you can ensure that your raised beds are optimized for success and yield abundant harvests.

Next, thorough **preparation** of the soil and raised bed structure sets the foundation for healthy growth and optimal plant development. Compost or well-rotted manure are examples of organic matter that can be added to soil to improve texture and drainage while also enriching it with vital nutrients. Additionally, ensuring proper bed construction and appropriate spacing between plants allows for better air circulation and reduces the risk of overcrowding, which can lead to disease and pest issues.

Paying close attention to the details is essential when planting. Take into account each plant's unique requirements, such as optimum sunshine exposure, water requirements, and compatibility with nearby plants. By selecting suitable varieties for your region and planting them at the right time, you give your plants the best chance to thrive and produce a bountiful harvest.

As your garden grows, don't overlook the crucial role of **parenting** your plants. Just like nurturing a child or a pet, your plants require care and attention. This includes regular watering, appropriate feeding, and diligent pruning. Watering deeply and consistently, especially during dry spells, helps promote strong root development and overall plant health. Feeding your plants with organic fertilizers or compost tea provides them with essential nutrients for robust growth and abundant yields. Pruning keeps your plants' size and form consistent, enhances airflow, and stops the spread of illnesses.

Strategic **plant pairings** can also have a significant impact on the health and productivity of your garden. Some plants have the innate capacity to deter pests or draw beneficial insects. By incorporating companion plants, you can create a harmonious ecosystem that deters pests, enhances pollination, and improves overall plant growth. Consider planting herbs like basil, marigold flowers, or aromatic plants like lavender, which can help repel pests and attract pollinators.

Lastly, don't neglect **protection**. Despite our best efforts, challenges may arise in the form of diseases, weeds, or adverse weather conditions. Regular monitoring of your plants is essential to identifying any signs of disease or pest infestations early on. Promptly remove any diseased plant parts to prevent the spread of pathogens. Using natural repellents like neem oil or implementing organic pest control strategies like introducing beneficial insects can help keep pests at bay. Additionally, mulching around your plants helps suppress weeds and conserve soil moisture while providing a protective barrier against extreme temperatures.

As we wrap up, I want to share what I'm growing in my own raised beds. This year I'm trying two new vegetables in a newly placed raised bed. My husband found a kit that is a perfect square made of galvanized steel for about $40 on sale at one of the garden centers in our area. We set it up specifically to grow broccoli and celery. I did plant cucumbers right next to that bed in another raised bed that we constructed from some landscape blocks that were left over from a project. I have since harvested the celery and broccoli and they were so flavorful! We are currently enjoying a variety of lettuce, grape and cherry tomatoes, cucumbers, and basil. We are now enjoying an abundant harvest of carrots, and a bigger variety of tomatoes. The joy of growing my own food and witnessing the transformation of seeds into flourishing plants is truly rewarding. Looking ahead to the next season, I'm excited to explore new varieties, experiment with other gardening techniques, and expand the range of vegetables and herbs in my raised beds.

Now, it's your turn to get started on creating your raised bed gardens. Choose the optimal site for your raised beds by considering elements like accessibility and sunshine exposure. Remember, you have what it takes to transform your garden into a beautiful, vibrant oasis that provides nourishment, beauty, and a connection to nature.

I appreciate you joining me on this fascinating gardening journey. May your raised beds flourish, your harvests be abundant, and your garden be a source of beauty, sustenance, and joy for years to come.

GLOSSARY

Adorn: Enhancing or embellishing something, like a garden or a plant, by adding decorative elements such as ornaments, flowers, or vibrant accents.

Aeration: Air- or oxygen-infusion is the process of introducing these elements to plant roots or soil.

Aesthetic appeal: The visual allure or pleasing appearance of something, such as a garden, a plant, or a landscape.

Alliums: A group of flowering plants that include well-known edible varieties like onions, garlic, and shallots.

Anaerobic pathogens: Diseases or microorganisms that survive in low-oxygen settings.

Anaerobic: Describing an environment or condition with low or absent levels of oxygen.

Aphid deterrent: Any substance or method used to repel or control aphids, which are small sap-sucking insects that can harm plants.

Biennial plants: Plants that mature in less than two years.

Biodiversity: The diversity of plant and animal species found in a particular habitat or location.

Biofungicides: Biological agents or substances utilized to manage fungal diseases in plants.

Carbon-rich: Pertaining to materials or substances containing a high concentration of carbon.

Chaff: The husks or outer coverings of seeds or grains that are separated during the threshing or processing of crops.

Cloches: Protective coverings or structures used in gardening to shield plants from adverse weather conditions or promote their growth.

Clogging potential: The likelihood or tendency of a material or substance to obstruct or block the flow of water, air, or other substances.

Clover: A leguminous plant from the Trifolium genus, known for its three-lobed leaves and small clustered flowers.

Companion planting: The practice of cultivating different plant species together to benefit each other in terms of pest control, nutrient uptake, pollination, or overall growth.

Compost: Nutrient-rich organic material produced through the decomposition of organic waste.

Containerized raised beds: Raised beds constructed by using containers or pots instead of building traditional raised beds directly on the ground.

Continuous production: An approach in gardening or farming where crops are grown and harvested in a staggered or successive manner.

Cotoneaster: A family of tiny trees and shrubs with flowers in the Rosaceae genus.

Cross-contamination: The transfer of pathogens, pests, or other harmful substances from one plant or area to another.

Dark green foliage: Describing the deep green coloration of leaves in plants.

Deadheading: Removing wasted or faded blooms from plants is a common procedure.

Debris: Any unwanted or discarded material, such as leaves, branches, or plant residues, which accumulates in the garden or landscape.

Decomposition: The process through which organic molecules naturally decompose into simpler compounds with the help of microbes.

Deep root penetration: The capacity of plant roots to penetrate the soil deeply.

Deep root system: A root system characterized by roots that extend deep into the soil profile.

Delicate stems: Describing the thin, fragile, or easily damaged stems of plants.

Diseased foliage: Foliage that is affected by diseases, such as fungal infections, bacterial diseases, viral infections, or other harmful conditions.

Dormancy: A stage of a plant's life cycle during which activity and growth slow down or momentarily stop, frequently under unfavorable climatic conditions.

Drought-tolerant plants: Plants that have the ability to withstand or adapt to extended periods of dryness or limited water availability.

Edible landscaping: The process of including food plants—such as fruits, vegetables, and herbs—into a landscape's planning and design.

Epiphytes: Plants that spread across the leaves of other plants, such as trees, without absorbing nutrition from their hosts.

Erosion control: Measures taken to prevent or minimize the loss of soil due to wind, water, or other environmental factors.

Espalier: A method used in horticulture to train and shape trees or plants, so they grow flat against a wall or trellis in a certain manner.

Etiolation: The process of plant growth in insufficient light, resulting in elongated, pale stems and reduced leaf development.

Fertilizer: Substances or materials that are incorporated into the soil or plants to supply them with vital nutrients that support growth and development.

Fungal pathogens: Microorganisms or pathogens that cause diseases in plants, such as fungi and fungal-like organisms.

Germination: A seed's initial growth and development into a new plant.

Grasscycling: The process of leaving grass clippings on a lawn after mowing them, in order to feed the soil with nutrients and organic matter.

Green manure: Legumes or cover crops are examples of plants that are produced, then added to the soil to increase organic matter and fertility.

Ground cover: Low-growing plants that spread across the ground, providing a dense carpet-like cover.

Hardening off: The process of gradually acclimating plants that were started indoors or in protected environments to the outdoor conditions.

Hardiness zone: A geographical area defined by the average annual minimum temperature, which helps determine the suitability of plants for a specific region.

Herbaceous plants: Plants that are not woody, have flexible stems, and usually die back to the ground in the winter.

Humus: Dark organic matter formed by the decomposition of plant and animal materials, contributing to soil fertility and structure.

Hybrid plants: Plants resulting from the crossbreeding of different species or varieties, often done to achieve desirable traits.

Invasive species: Non-native plants that have the potential to spread rapidly and outcompete native vegetation, causing harm to the ecosystem.

Macroelements: Essential nutrients required by plants in relatively large quantities, including nitrogen, phosphorus, potassium, calcium, magnesium, and sulfur.

Microelements: Trace elements or micronutrients are essential nutrients that plants need in minute amounts.

Mulch: A layer of protection made of compost, wood chips, or straw that is spread over the top of the soil to control temperature, prevent weed growth, and conserve moisture.

Native plants: Plants that are native to a particular area or ecosystem and have evolved to do well in that environment.

Nitrogen-fixing plants: Plants have the capacity to change atmospheric nitrogen into a form that can be utilized by other plants, typically legumes.

Organic gardening: A gardening technique that relies on organic, sustainable methods rather than synthetic pesticides, fertilizers, and other growing aids.

Perennials: Plants that have a lifespan of more than two years and frequently blossom and generate seeds throughout that time.

pH: A measurement of a substance's acidity or alkalinity, with a pH of 7 considered neutral, anything lower or higher being acidic.

Pollination: Pollen transfer refers to the movement of pollen from a flower's male reproductive organs to its female reproductive organs, which results in fertilization and seed development.

Seed saving: The act of gathering and saving plant seeds for later planting with the goal of maintaining genetic diversity and adaptation.

Soil amendment: Materials added to soil to improve its physical properties, nutrient content, or water-holding capacity, such as compost, peat moss, or perlite.

Trellis: A framework or structure, often made of wood or metal, used to support climbing or trailing plants.

Water-wise gardening: A gardening approach that emphasizes water conservation and efficient water use, through strategies such as mulching, proper irrigation, and selecting drought-tolerant plants.

Weed control: The management and prevention of unwanted plants, commonly referred to as weeds, which compete with desired plants for resources.

Other books by this author:

Soil science for beginners
Your Step-By-Step Guide To Improve Soil For Optimal Crop
Health, Maximize Yield And Create Pest-Resistant Plants
With Organic Methods, Even If You're New to Gardening!

Companion Planting For Beginners
A Guide To Pairing Fruits, Vegetables, Flowers & Herbs For
Nutrient-Rich Soil, Higher Yields & Natural Pest Control –
No Green Thumb Required!

Greenhouse Gardening For Beginners
A Practical Guide To Choose & Maintain A Greenhouse,
Grow Pest-Resistant Plants & Harvest Organic Produce –
No Experience Required!

Garden Log Journal

REFERENCES

2.5 Reading a Seed Packet | Cornell Garden-Based Learning. (n.d.). Gardening.cals.cornell.edu. https://gardening.cals.cornell.edu/lessons/project-s-o-w-seeds-of-wonder-food-gardening-with-justice-in-mind/unit-2-gardening-with-gratitude/2-5-reading-a-seed-packet/.

Angelo. (2020, July 23). *Three Simple Soil Tests to Determine What Type of Soil You Have.* Deep Green Permaculture. https://deepgreenpermaculture.com/2020/07/23/three-simple-soil-tests-to-determine-what-type-of-soil-you-have/.

BrightView. (2017). *4 Signs You are Overwatering Your Plants.* Brightview.com. https://www.brightview.com/resources/article/four-signs-you-are-over watering-your-plants.

Burke, N. (2022, March 17). *Where to Put Your Raised Beds — How to Choose the Ideal Location • Gardenary.* Gardenary. https://www.gardenary.com/blog/where-to-put-your-raised-beds-how-to-choose-the-ideal-location.

Confucius quote. (n.d.). A-Z Quotes. https://www.azquotes.com/quote/950765.

DNP, L. W. a. C. (2022). Dig into the benefits of gardening. *Mayo Clinic Health System.* https://www.mayoclinichealthsystem.org/hometown-health/speaking-of-health/dig-into-the-benefits-of-gardening.

Faires, N. (2017, March 21). *10 Excellent Reasons to Use Raised Beds in Your Garden.* Eartheasy Guides & Articles. https://learn.eartheasy.com/articles/10-excellent-reasons-to-use-raised-beds-in-your-garden/.

Gardening Quotes. (n.d.). *Inspirational Quotes at BrainyQuote.* https://www.brainyquote.com/topics/gardening-quotes 2.

Growing Your Own | The three sisters / RHS Gardening. (n.d.). Www.rhs.org.uk. https://www.rhs.org.uk/advice/grow-your-own/features/three-sisters.

Hold the flowers. (2022, March 6). Thebreadandbuddha. https://www.the-breadandbuddha.com/single-post/hold-the-flowers#:~

How and When to Transplant Seedlings: 6 Easy Steps to Transplanting Success |

Permaculture Gardens. (n.d.). Growmyownfood.com. https://growmyown food.com/how-and-when-to-transplant-seedlings/.

How to Make a Hoophouse on a Raised Bed. (n.d.). Grow Organic. https://www. groworganic.com/blogs/articles/how-to-make-a-hoophouse-on-a-raised-bed.

Howell, J. (2021, January 27). *How to Build a Wood Raised Garden Bed.* Garden Gate. https://www.gardengatemagazine.com/articles/projects/all/how-to-build-a-wood-raised-garden-bed/.

Jenni. (2022, March 8). *What Are the Best Flowers for Raised Beds.* The Housist. https://thehousist.com/gardening/what-are-the-best-flowers-for-raised-beds/.

Jill. (2022, October 28). *6 Raised Bed Irrigation Options for Home Gardens.* The Beginner's Garden. https://journeywithjill.net/gardening/2022/10/28/raised-bed-irrigation-options/.

Jonathon.David.Madore. (n.d.). *Should You Mulch A Raised Garden Bed? (Plus 9 Organic Mulches).* GreenUpSide. https://greenupside.com/should-you-mulch-a-raised-garden-bed-plus-9-organic-mulches/.

Lettuce: Looseleaf Blend. Warminster, Pennslvania: Burpee Garden Products Co, 2020.

Malin, Z. (2021, May 21). *How to plant in raised garden beds, according to experts.* NBC News. https://www.nbcnews.com/select/shopping/best-raised-garden-beds-ncna1268061.

Mariotti, T. (2022, September 5). *Gardening Statistics (2022).* RubyHome.com. https://www.rubyhome.com/blog/gardening-stats/.

NSW Government. (2017). *Plant nutrients in the soil.* Www.dpi.nsw.gov.au. https://www.dpi.nsw.gov.au/agriculture/soils/soil-testing-and-analysis/plant-nutrients.

Published, S. W. (2021, November 27). *Best plants with winter berries: 15 plants for adding color.* Gardeningetc.com. https://www.gardeningetc.com/advice/plants-with-winter-berries.

Pugle, M. (2022, June 30). *Is Stress The Number One Killer?* Psych Central. https://psychcentral.com/stress/is-stress-the-number-one-killer.

Rumi Quote: "And don't think the garden loses its ecstasy in winter. It's quiet, but the roots are down there riotous." (n.d.). https://quotefancy.com/quote/

904119/Rumi-And-don-t-think-the-garden-loses-its-ecstasy-in-winter-It-s-quiet-but-the-roots-are.

Saleem, M. I. (n.d.). *BUILDING RAISED GARDEN BEDS WITH RECYCLED MATERIALS*. Bed Gardening. https://www.bedgardening.com/building-raised-garden-beds-with-recycled-materials/.

Schipani, S. (2019, September 26). *How to prepare a raised garden bed for winter*. Hello Homestead. https://hellohomestead.com/how-to-prepare-a-raised-garden-bed-for-winter/.

September 1, J. C. |, & 2000. (2000, September 1). *Nine Keys to Plant Disease Prevention*. Brooklyn Botanic Garden. https://www.bbg.org/article/disease_prevention.

Team, C. (2021, August 24). Fresh Insights Into The Growing Home Garden Trend. *Collab Fund*. https://collabfund.com/blog/fresh-insights-into-the-growing-home-garden-trend/.

The world counts. (n.d.). https://www.theworldcounts.com/challenges/planet-earth/state-of-the-planet/when-will-the-world-run-out-of-water.

Walliser, J. (2018, February 6). *Identifying Garden Pests: How to Figure Out Who's Eating Your Plants*. Savvy Gardening. https://savvygardening.com/identifying-garden-pests/.

Wells, K. (2019). Why do gardeners live longer? *Wellness Mama®*. https://wellnessmama.com/natural-home/gardeners-live-longer/#:~

IMAGE REFERENCE

Damiani, M (2023) Photo/Broccoli After Rain.

Damiani, M (2023) Photo/Cedar 4 x 8 RBG.

Damiani, M (2023) Photo/Frame RBG

Damiani, M (2023) Photo/Inside Corner

Damiani, M (2023) Photo/Metal RBG.

Damiani, M (2023) Photo/Outside Corner

Damiani, M (2023) Photo/Planning.

Damiani, M (2023) Photo/Seed Packet.

Damiani, M (2023) Photo/Soil & Compost.

Damiani, M (2023) Photo/Stone Stacking.

Damiani, M (2023) Photo/Waterfall.

Palozzi, F (Circa 1970s) Garden Michelle & Frost Protection.

Palozzi, F (Circa 1970s) Garden brother & dogs.

Sikdar, A. (2017). https://unsplash.com/photos/LoGnr-w1D8E.